KEN McCORMACK'S
DERRY
VOLUME III

FEATURING
The Lady in Black
& Other Curious Tales

Colmcille Press

Published October 2024 by
Colmcille Press
Ráth Mór Centre
Derry
Northern Ireland
BT48 0LZ
www.colmcillepress.com

Cover shipwreck picture by kind permission of Victorian Web
Portrait of Sir Ian Fraser by kind permission of Queen's University Belfast

Produced in association with Foyle Books and The John Bryson Foundation and with kind assistance from the Heritage Lottery Recovery Fund.

Foyle Books | The John Bryson Foundation |  MAOIN DUALCHAIS HERITAGE FUND

© 2024 in text Ken McCormack

The moral right of the author has been asserted.

ISBN 978 1 914009 44 0

All rights reserved. No part of this publication may be reproduced or transmitted in any form or by any means, electronic or mechanical, including photocopy, recording, or any information storage or retrieval system, without permission in writing from the publisher. The book is sold subject to the condition that it shall not, by way of trade or otherwise, be lent, re-sold or otherwise circulated without the publisher's prior consent in any form of binding or cover other than that in which it is published and without a similar condition including this condition being imposed on the subsequent purchaser.

*This book is dedicated to my parents
Phyllis and John, my brother John,
his wife Helen and their families,
and my brother Bernard
and his wife Andree*

By the Author

Following the Foyle

Ken McCormack's Derry
Vol.1 – Heroes, Villains and Ghosts
Vol. 2 – The Black Bird and the Canary
Vol. 3 – The Lady in Black

A Memoir of Glendermott Valley

Winter Ghosts – Series 1

Winter Ghosts – Series 2

The Haunting

On the Subject of Love (City of Culture selected play)

Introduction

Ken McCormack studied at the University of Ulster, Queen's University, the Open University and the Derry and Belfast Technical Colleges. Originally in telecommunications, part of his work involved hazardous sea crossings by open boat to Rathlin Island.

During advanced studies, he took masters degrees in Education and Philosophy, and a Higher Diploma in Counselling.

He moved into teaching in the mid-sixties, remaining there until his retirement. In between times he was asked to join the newly-established BBC Radio Foyle, where for years he presented programmes and made documentaries. He continues to be involved in radio work.

Ken has written five books and presently is co-authoring three others; he has written several plays including The Haunting and On the Subject of Love, which was the chosen play for Derry City of Culture.

He has travelled widely in Europe, China and North Africa and spent time in the Lower Allegheny Mountains in America on the hunt for a family ancestor.

Ken lives in Derry. His interests are football, cricket and books.
The Lady in Black is edited by Diana Kilpatrick

John McCormack (1945-2024)

On the 3rd of December 1945 when I had returned home for lunch from the Waterside Boys' School folk said to me go upstairs to your mother she has a surprise for you. Up the stairs I went to the front room and there was my mother sitting up in bed smiling and holding a white shawl that was wrapped around a beautiful new-born baby. This was John who had come into the world two hours earlier and destined to be my beloved brother until his passing in May 2024. John turned out to be the darling boy in our family – the neighbours and all who got to know him loved him. We were playmates growing up as children, then in football, cricket and fishing before John moved through St. Columb's College and unto Queen's University where he also played football. Even though at times we were not together the brotherly connection was always there. John came across the same to everybody – friendly, mild-mannered, open, generous and welcoming. I never knew him do a nasty act or say anything bad about anybody. In time he would marry his loving wife Helen and produce a devoted family – Jacqueline. Theresa, Martin, Kenneth, Helina and John. He was a well-loved teacher at St. Colman's Strabane, where he became Vice-Principal and he excelled at golf, fishing and football. John followed me into Radio Foyle for a spell and then wrote for the Waterside Voices. In our years of retirement we walked every day and it was during this time that he told me about a tale he was working on – the *Cambria* tragedy. It became the flagship story and title of this present book – *The Lady in Black*. During his illness John passed his file to me and I was able to tell him I was working on it but, it is his story and I see it as a tribute to him.

Some folk in life give one a reason to be and a reason to do – this was John for me – my inspiration and quite simply the best person I have ever known.

Contents

LET FATE DECIDE
- The Lady in Black — 12
- Interview with a Psychic — 21
- Carl's Fateful Journey — 26
- The Enagh Aviator – Magnificent Man in his Flying Machine — 34
- The Mystery of the Unmarked Grave — 37

NEVER FORGOTTEN
- The Magical Hats of Madame Beck — 48
- Lyster's Golden Touch — 54
- The Watts and the *Whiskey Man* — 59
- The Killing of Lord Leitrim — 64
- The Lady in the Moon — 73

STRANGE TALES TO TELL
- The Mystery of the Viaduct Disaster — 80
- The Cabina Affair — 87
- Down at the Ivy Church — 92
- Malady at the Bridge — 97
- The Secrets of St. Columb's Park House — 101

SO MANY HORRID GHOSTS
- The Case of the Singing Ghost — 110
- Things That Go Bump in the Night — 113
- Country Ghosts — 117
- A Haunting in Fanad — 121
- The Ghost of the White Horse Inn — 125

TWIST IN THE TALE
- Silver Flash — 130
- The Dawning of the Day — 135
- The Taming of Kerry Blue — 143
- The Wire — 150
- How Many Miles to Babylon? — 157

CAMEOS

The Honeymoon Tree	166
Rudyard Kipling in Derry	167
The Mysterious Lady of Boom Hall	168
Good Morning Your Reverence…!	170
The Mystery of the Dead Boy on a Dolphin	172
Derry's Legendary Ballerina	174
Derry Hosts a Famous Ship… and, a Medal for a Cat!	175
Can it be Believed?	177
Buckie O'Boyle's Gold	178
A Whiskey Man's Fate	180
The Local Hero Who Travelled the Arctic Wastes	181
The Loneliness Stone	183
Develop a Limp	184
A Magnificent Man *Without* His Flying Machine	185

EXCERPTS FROM MY DIARY

On Top of Sacre Coeur – and a Fright!	188
'Sure the Young Fella 'ill Have a Drop Too.'	189
Hazardous Journey	190
My Books Are in the River, Sir!	191
Becoming a Broadcaster	192
Dr. Who's Scarf – Evening News Radio Foyle	193
A Nice Little Earner… !	194
The Man Who Slept with a Queen	195
On the Beach with Josef Locke	195
Seventh Son of a Seventh Son	196
The Remarkable Cecily Mackworth	197
The Golden Buddha and Me	198

ACKNOWLEDGEMENTS 200

GALLERY 203

Let Fate Decide

The Lady in Black

On the evening of Friday 21 October 1870 William Cane, out for a stroll on Bushfoot beach near Bushmills and not far from the Giant's Causeway, is in for a shock he will not forget in a hurry. After a fierce storm on the previous Wednesday night, talk is of a shipwreck, so it is no surprise to find flotsam and jetsam along the length of the shore. Yet what especially takes his eye is a dark shape cast up on the tideline. To his horror what he comes upon is the body of a young woman lying there as if curled up asleep yet dead to the world. There is no identification as to who this might be; the only remarkable feature is her beautiful full length black silk dress. Nearby is an empty ship's lifeboat with the words *SS Cambria,* Glasgow, on its side. Immediately the alarm goes up – has she come from the shipwreck and what circumstances have brought her to be cast up on this wild and beautiful place? It is a sensation far and wide and gives rise to the legendary tale that has come to be known as the mystery of *The Lady in Black…*

'All aboard that's' goin' aboard!'

Saturday evening 8 October 1870, and affairs are at fever pitch on New York's East River Pier 20 as the last of the passengers board the Anchor Line's metal steamship *SS Cambria* bound for Moville and Glasgow. At the deck rail watching the crowds milling around on the quay is passenger John McGartland, aged twenty-five, and he hails a young crewman walking past him on the deck. A neat, good-looking and well-mannered lad, he is dressed in a smart navy tunic with brass buttons, gold epaulettes and fine white flannels.

'Hey son what time are we leavin'?'

'There's no tide till midnight. It'll be into the wee hours of Sunday morning – the ninth of October.'

'I like your uniform. Are you the captain?' says McGartland joking with the youngster.

'Captain? Sure I'm only sixteen. Robert Robinson, trainee steward at your service.'

'I'm John McGartland travellin' steerage and bound for Mountfield outside Omagh. I'll be off at Moville. You're not a Jock with an accent like that young fella?'

'I'm from Derry – almost a year with the Anchor Line. I've a couple of crossings under my belt – even served at the captain's table on the way out.'

'Aren't you the one! Who's the Captain anyway?'

'Captain Carnighan. He's the best. They say he'll be the commodore one day.'

Suddenly McGartland's attention is drawn to a woman down on the quay struggling with her luggage.

'Hey! Would ye look at that. Lady in black – what a stunner!'

She looks to be in her early twenties, is of average height, attractive and stylishly dressed in black but very pale. 'She'll need help. I'll give her a hand – see you later,' calls young Robinson dashing off.

He sees the lady safely installed in her cabin – she is travelling intermediate; first class is at the stern; intermediate or second is next; then steerage towards the bow; all accommodation is in tip top condition since the *Cambria* is just a year old. Slim and elegant with a single funnel and three masts for her sails, she has the name of being a great ship with a really pleasant crew and excellent catering facilities.

Eventually with all the passengers aboard and the last of the cargo, mostly grain, loaded, the gangplank is withdrawn. Like an athlete limbering up, last checks are made; officers are busy on the bridge and the crew at their stations. Finally ropes are cast off,

Cambria's 400 horsepower engine roars into life and with a judder she eases herself away from the quay into the tide, which is already rushing down the Hudson River and into the East Estuary. Soon they will be leaving Manhattan and Brooklyn behind – and also the first signs of the mighty Brooklyn Bridge whose building has just commenced. On the waterway it is still as busy as day; ferries are crisscrossing everywhere and both sides are lined with clippers from all parts of the world.

There are cheers from the quayside and waves from the deck as the *Cambria* gives three blasts of her horn and moves into midstream.

'Wind's west and fully behind us Captain,' says the mate.

'Then set us full steam east and go to canvas as well,' orders Carnighan.

With a strong wind steam vessels with sails can make speeds of fifteen knots and more and *Cambria* can reach this easily. At almost 2000 tons she is 324 feet long and 35 across. The crew total eighty and her complement of passengers is 102 for this particular trip.

Two days out and Robert Robinson gets his first chance to have a word with John McGartland in steerage. The place is pretty basic but comfortable with wooden bunks along the sides and separate sections for families and single girls.

'I brought you some bread and apples,' smiles Robert.

'You're one decent lad,' replies the grateful McGartland. 'Food here's tight enough.'

'Remember that lady, the one in black that I helped with her luggage?' asks Robert.

'Aye, some stunner she was.'

'Well…she's in an intermediate cabin – second class.'

'Lucky for some.'

'She's very nice. Told me she's not been well, going home to somewhere near Enniskillen. But…'

'But what?'

'I checked on the passenger list for a woman of her description. She's not on it!'

'Ye mean she's a ghost or somethin'? Did ye get her name?"

'We're not allowed to ask. But it's strange.'

'You sea folk are all the same, plain superstitious. Anythin' out of the ordinary an' the world's comin' to an end.'

'Mmm…we'll see…I've a feeling about it…'

Robert goes about his business and despite choppy seas *Cambria* makes good progress so that in just over eight days she is well across. However, on Tuesday evening 18th October the stiff wind from the west starts rising into a gale and still continues to get stronger throughout Wednesday.

'Something about storms building I don't like,' grumbles the captain. 'Ease our canvas, Mister Mate.'

William Johnston, the chief mate, is a young man of twenty-five years and highly respected throughout the Anchor Line -'Aye! Aye! Captain,' he replies and the call goes out to take in the sails.

Carnighan looks at his chart – 'Tory Island should be coming up but where is it? This rain's so torrential.'

'There sir, to starboard! Just a flicker, it's the Tory light all right.'

'Good! Helmsman take us fifteen points north so we can follow the coast to the Foyle – and tell the steward to ready the party for Derry, twenty-three off at Moville.'

Moville is on the River Foyle estuary with Derry about twenty miles upstream.

'Captain, sir!' interrupts the mate. 'Before the Foyle, Inishtrahull Island just off Malin Head is on our track. We need to give it a wide berth.'

'I know Mister Mate. I can hardly see with the spray and the downpour but that looks like it now.'

The black menacing shape of Inishtrahull is just about visible but no light can be seen.

Nearing ten o'clock the waves are thirty feet high and lashing the *Cambria*; the wind is reaching hurricane force and the noise is unbearable; worse still the vessel is yawing and pitching and with no visibility control is almost impossible.'

'Steady! Bring her west and another point north, helmsman,' urges Carnighan.

'Aye Captain but it's forcing us landwards.'

'Keep at it or we'll be into that bloody island,' barks the Captain.

'Main danger's the Tor Rocks on the other side of Inishtrahull, Captain,' calls the mate.

But it is too late.

Before they can utter another word, a giant wave lifts the *Cambria* as if it were matchwood and smashes its starboard bow into the fearsome black mass of Tor Beg rock just beyond Inishtrahull.

There is an enormous thud and folk are tossed off their feet throughout the ship.

'My God, Mister Mate we've struck! Our bow plates are gone. Sea's flooding in.'

Both men look at one another and both know the *SS Cambria* is doomed.

'Sound the alarm! Call all hands – lifeboats! Lifeboats!' cries the Captain.

'Lifeboat stations!' The call goes out across the vessel, with the crew dashing to all parts to gather the passengers. Soon bewildered and panic-stricken groups are lining up for the boats as best they can for the *Cambria* is pitching wildly. It is fearsome, terrifying beyond belief.

It is now almost eleven o'clock and the sea is like a boiling cauldron as the crew prepare to lower the lifeboats. One, two, three, filled to capacity are lowered and vanish into the darkness but the screams of folk in the wind indicate their fate – capsized. John McGartland queues for the fourth boat and remarkably as fate would have it there beside him is the lady in black, a shawl about her shoulders but shivering nonetheless.

'Quickly! Quickly!' urges the crew and suddenly McGartland notices Robert Robinson helping folk into the boat. 'Robert!

Robert! Come on board with us!' he cries.

'Please young man!' begs the woman.

Robert thinks about it but hesitates before calling, 'I can't. I can't! My duty's to the passengers!'

McGartland tries to grab him but he shakes free and looks at them; they look at him and in that split second there is no sound, no pandemonium; no wild ocean for them; they are caught in some timeless place, strangers yet held together in a human bond. But suddenly it is shattered as a crewman manhandles McGartland and the woman into the boat.

Their last glance is of the boy waving a farewell from the *Cambria* as the backwash from the vessel sweeps the lifeboat away. Yet the living hell of that night is far from over, for suddenly the lifeboat is broadsided by one wave and then tipped over by another so that the full complement of souls are tossed out into the ocean and swallowed up in an instant.

Nevertheless, it is not finished for McGartland. Miraculously he surfaces and whether he had been unconscious or not he finds himself in the water but with one arm over the lifeboat gunwale. With difficulty he scrambles into the vessel holding on for grim death for it is heaving to and fro, like a being possessed. Then as he takes stock the sight before his eyes makes his blood run cold for there lying halfway along the boat is the lady – the lady in black and she is dead.

Ghastly as this is, his living nightmare is still not over, for, with the ordeal of the sinking ship and being exposed to the wet and cold conditions he is falling in and out of consciousness. Then as the time slips into the small hours the wicked edge of the storm abates so that McGartland now in a sort of stupor drifts about knowing not where he is and worst of all unable to help himself. Yet fate has another card to play. About 2:30am on Thursday morning the steam boat *Enterprise,* a Derry vessel venturing home from Liverpool as the storm subsides, spots his drifting lifeboat near the entrance to Lough Foyle. Although the sea is still rough, eventually

Captain Gillespie of the *Enterprise* manages to put alongside it and John Bradley, his mate, is able to get aboard the lifeboat in highly dangerous conditions, and help McGartland on to the *Enterprise*.

'What about the woman?' shouts Bradley to his captain.

'Too dangerous,' calls Gillespie. 'You'll be washed away if you don't get back on board now!'

The mate does so just as a vicious current sweeps the lifeboat away and off it goes carrying the remains of the lady in black – a grisly scene, for the ocean has a ghostly luminescence about it.

'Such a pity we could do nothing,' says the mate as he watches the lifeboat vanish into the gloom.

'If I know the tides about here, and I reckon I do, she'll be washed up near the Giant's Causeway,' replies Captain Gillespie.

Never were truer words spoken as William Cane the stroller on Bushfoot beach discovered on the Friday evening mentioned at the beginning of our tale. And now with the weekend upon them, officials at Bushmills are obliged to hold an inquest as soon as possible and have the woman's remains buried quickly after that. Yet the Anchor Line can find no details of her on their passenger list – a fact that young Robert Robinson had already mentioned to John McGartland when he met him in steerage. So there is mystery. Without doubt the woman joined the *Cambria* in New York so how could it be?

News goes out across the countryside about the unidentified body but in days when newspapers and word of mouth are the main ways of informing folk there is no response.

And now the plot thickens. The woman's remains are placed in the Bushmills mortuary and on Saturday afternoon 22 October a short inquest returns a verdict of 'Unknown; found drowned'. This enables a burial to take place but with that another curious twist in this tale is about to take place. James Gilmour, a farmer of Banagh, near Kesh, County Fermanagh only hearing late in the day about the *Cambria* disaster says he thinks his daughter had travelled on it. But Anchor Line officials find no record of a woman of that

Interview with a Psychic

Is there anybody there?

I was on the quest of a rather delicate subject so I must admit to being a little nervous when I knocked on the psychic's door.

There was no response.

It was on a chilly, damp October afternoon some years back in one of those unending streets of red brick houses huddled around Queen's University Belfast. My unease was down to a feeling that there was a mystique about what psychics do, thanks mainly to seeing programmes on television about messages from beyond the grave – not everyone's cup of tea of course and certainly not to be confused with ghosts, though one might be forgiven for thinking they are not a million miles apart.

However, to clarify the matter of what a psychic was I had checked my dictionary and found – *a psychic is a person who claims to use extrasensory perception (ESP) to identify information hidden from the normal senses and particularly relating to that which is in the afterlife; many psychics are advocates of the world of spiritualism.*

I knocked again and there was still no reply. 'Another day,' I thought and, a little relieved, was about to turn away when I heard footsteps in the hall and the door opened. There in front of me was a tall slim man, seventy-ish I guessed, hair greying and brushed back; altogether very well presented – friendly too.

'Richard Gibson?' I enquired.

'Indeed I am. Well Dick actually, not Richard…and you must be Ken. Do come in.'

It was as easy as that. He led me upstairs to a little flat comfortably furnished and with a welcoming fire. I had explained already on the phone that I was doing a series for BBC Northern Ireland on 'out of the ordinary' topics and, having read his name in a local newspaper where he had been consulted for his experience as a psychic, I was hoping he might contribute to a programme on spiritualism.

I was soon to learn that Dick was a man of considerable experience. He had given his life to spiritualism from an early age, knew most of its leading personalities while in England and having obtained all the necessary Spiritualists' Union qualifications returned to Belfast as Dick Gibson CSNU, the first Spiritualist minister in Ireland.

Spiritualism, I discovered, was a church and a philosophy for living, since messages and meanings were conveyed through it. As far as I could see, it did not predict the future like the Greeks' Oracle of Delphi, or the Romans' dissecting animal entrails, or indeed cards, tea cups or crystal balls. Apparently folk often mistook clairvoyance in spiritualism as foretelling what is to come when certainly it was not this.

According to Dick, 'Clairvoyance was the ability to see in a clear, rational and objective way, and the psychic as trance-medium, the best means to receive and relay messages from the spirit world. Thus the holding of séances with the medium and a group of people.'

Another feature is that the Spiritualists' Union believes in healing – spiritual healing from the almighty that may lead to physical healing of folk who are ill.

As my interview with Dick continued on that afternoon it became more intriguing. He began to reveal the spiritual energies that worked through him personally. Firstly, for discovery or diagnosis he had an American native Indian spirit with the splendid name of *Soft Wind in the Tall Pine Trees;* then a French spirit guide for clear seeing and finally as much as I could comprehend a German doctor – Schmitt – whom Dick described as brilliant. This trio guided Dick in spiritual healing and advertisements in

Belfast newspapers from the 1940s onwards show him as active in the many branches of Spiritualism.

I have to say that Dick was very open about everything – very detailed, very informative and very generous with his time.

Finally, I wanted to know what the afterlife was like – was there any way a psychic could see or perhaps even witness the world beyond? Here I felt we were bordering on challenging territory. Dick talked of a *Gatekeeper* guarding the entry to the world beyond and how to journey within it if one dared and, as the hair rose on the back of my neck, I sensed it better to go no further.

Darkness was closing in on that October evening – we could have chatted all night but before leaving he gave me the names of three contacts in London to further help with my programme. With that I took my leave of this nice and most helpful man with the promise to keep in touch.

My next stop was London and with three visits to make it was becoming quite an adventure. Firstly, to Tony Ortzen, editor of the *Psychic News* from the 1980s. I recall walking across London's Cambridge Circus on the way to the *Psychic News* HQ and being just as nervous as I was when I had first contacted Dick Gibson. Yet once again nothing but a warm welcome. Tony was highly articulate and very confident about the afterlife. 'What is it like?' I asked and straightaway he answered, 'Not just one place but many – a world of wonder where there is no death and the pain of human baggage is left behind. I have absolutely no fear of dying whatsoever.'

Spiritualism had its roots in 1848 with the Fox sisters Kate and Margaret. It flourished in Victorian times but fell into disrepute when some séances were found to be fraudulent. An upswing happened with the loss of life in the First World War when parents, sweethearts and families sought answers or tried to make sense of where their young loved ones had gone after death on the battlefield – did they still exist after passing from life? One of the chief protagonists for Spiritualism at the time was Sir Arthur Conan Doyle of Sherlock Holmes fame. His fascination with the supernatural grew after his son Kingsley and his younger brother Innes, battle-weary from service in World War I, died amid the worldwide influenza pandemic shortly after returning home. Another advocate was Sir Oliver Lodge, a famous physicist who had lost his son Raymond at Ypres; he claimed to have had conversations with him afterwards through a medium. Both these men had as many supporters as critics and both were often accused of being deluded. So I asked Tony Ortzen was it not just imagination at work?

'Not at all, 'said he, 'I've heard from too many spirit guides – and they live there!'

My next call was with Wilfred Watts, a Spiritualist minister and member of the Society for Psychical Research. 'It is right that those who've passed can communicate with us,' Wilfred told me, 'and it is the case that sometimes messages are passed that are not yet known at the time in the world of the living. The messages come to me as mental pictures in my mind.'

Finally, I found myself knocking on the door of the London Spiritual Mission and getting a warm greeting from the secretary Rosalind Cattanach. This was a delightful, peaceful place with a wonderful auditorium. 'Spiritualism is service to mankind and by this we serve God,' said Rosalind. Her two beautiful dogs sat at our feet and it occurred to me to ask 'What happens to pets. Do they go to the other side as well?' Rosalind gave a beaming smile 'They certainly do,' said she, 'Even at this moment they are running around us!'

I was not aware of that though I must say Rosalind's smile spoke of her great belief.

I could not finish without mention of a treat that Dick Gibson had in store for me when I went to see him on the visit I had promised. 'Let's get in your car and go up to Malone,' said he and in a few minutes we were outside a large house in Belfast's well-to-do district. He obviously knew the place well for he walked straight through the house to the back and into a large greenhouse. Seated at an easel in the middle was a bearded, good-looking man, whom

Dick introduced as Raymond Piper. It struck me immediately that it was *the* Raymond Piper, one of Northern Ireland's top artists – a man of many talents – artist, sculptor, teacher and musician. I had seen his work on the walls of the Wellington Park hotel and he had staged countless exhibitions.

We had a very pleasant chat about our interests and I got round to asking how he had first come to notice his flair for art. 'It was when I was a young boy,' he told me. 'I used to explore the Cave Hill, which I grew to love. Gradually, everything about me began to take on an aura – plants and trees – there were vibrant colours and intensities. It wasn't overpowering but it was there and I felt very enriched by it. My creative talent sprang from that.'

Whatever it was, it was special for Raymond Piper (d. 2007) for he came to be very highly regarded. It also explained his friendship with Dick Gibson, for Dick had told me that he too could detect auras in the form of coloured glowing energies around people. So it looks as if they had much to chat about.

Anyway my exploration into the world of Spiritualism was nearing completion. I kept in contact with Dick by phone but one day while in Belfast I decided to call on him only to be told he had moved. Eventually I found him living in what I guessed was a 'Fold' on the outskirts of the city. It took ages to get a response to my knock and when at last he appeared *I knew in the way that one knows* that he was not at all well – indeed had gone downhill badly. Unusually, he did not want to chat much and sadly that was the last I ever saw of him.

There was however one final surprise. After my radio programme, with which I was very pleased, out of the blue I was amazed to receive a copy of the *Spiritualist News*, the monthly national newspaper. Where had it come from? That I cannot say – but I can reveal that we (the BBC) got bold front page leading headlines – 'Spiritualism's Case is Heard in Northern Ireland!'

It was an excellent piece yet all I can add is that Spiritualism or not, I did not sense *that* coming!

Carl's Fateful Journey

*'... Fate? No one alive has ever escaped it,
I tell you – it's born with us.'*
(Homer; *The Iliad*)

Visitors to Rathlin Island's St. Thomas's graveyard cannot fail to be puzzled by a lonely tombstone that reads:

*Erected by His Highness
Prince Albrecht of Waldeck
In memory of his faithful servant
Carl Piel
Who died September 23rd.
1868
Aged 26 years*

Herein lies a tale of the extraordinary friendship between two young men where one gave his life in the service of the other – as we shall see the tombstone speaks the most curious of messages and knowing Rathlin Island well as I do it has always intrigued me greatly.

Now there are two versions of this story. The first starts in an odd almost fairytale way. Back in the 1800s a newspaper report talked of a mysterious youth being washed up on the shore of Rathlin Island off Ireland's North coast. Rathlin Island is 'L' shaped, some seven miles long and less than two miles wide.

The incident happened in 1860; the boy's age being about

nineteen years coming on twenty. It was said he was soaking wet, was suffering from exposure and that his small boat was flooded. At this time Rathlin Island had some 450 inhabitants most of them cared for spiritually and otherwise by the parish priest, and the rector of St Thomas' Protestant Church the Reverend Thomas Gage owner of the island who lived in the manor house near the shore.

Those who discovered the youth carried him to the parish priest who over the next few days brought him back to health. The only problem was that he could not speak English; what better then than to take him to the Reverend Gage at the manor house, thought the priest – surely some of the well-schooled Gage daughters would understand his strange language. And there were daughters aplenty at the Gage's – eight to be precise along with three boys. So, the recovering youth was transferred to the manor house and one can only imagine the excitement when this young man appeared – very good looking, polite and well-mannered. Yet none of the family could make any headway with his language until they tried French, which he understood quite well.

Gradually it became apparent that he was German and called Albrecht, a student at the University of Bonn and of the family that ruled the German Principality of Waldeck and Pyrmont. He had come to visit the Giant's Causeway and having taken out a boat to better view the Causeway's curious stones was swept away towards the nearby Rathlin Island by a fierce current.

This could well validate the tale for at the time folk would often view the Causeway from boats on the water. Thackeray, the writer, records doing so some eighteen years earlier in 1842 – all very well in fine weather of course but given the wrong conditions this stretch was one of the most dangerous of Irish coastal waters; the hazard caused by the meeting of the Irish Sea and the Atlantic Ocean between Ireland and Scotland and known as the *Sea of Moyle*. It was and still remains famous in Irish mythology for the story of the *Swans of Lir;* unpredictable vicious currents and counter currents abound in these waters.

Centuries earlier St Columba and his disciples made this perilous journey on the way from Derry to Iona, their ears strained for the roar of the *Coire Brecan*, the terrifying whirlpool off the Scottish shore that could appear without warning and draw boats to their doom. I can vouch for the dangers myself for as a young telecommunications engineer I often made trips to Rathlin Island by open boat – many of them hair-raising; indeed frequently we came dangerously close to Scotland because of the strength of the tides.

Young Albrecht was treated like a lord at the manor house. In those days Rathlin Island was quite isolated with journeys only by rowing boat. So it took time for his return to the mainland. It is often said that love can grow in an instant and while all the Gage girls were beauties it seems that a special attraction grew straightaway between the young German and the youngest of the Gages called Dorothea – known as Dora within the family. Not surprising then that when Albrecht settled back home he dispatched a letter of thanks to the Rathlin parish priest and enclosed an invitation for the Gage girls to come to a grand celebration in Bonn, a beautiful old world German city and birthplace of Beethoven. It took a while for the girls to decide to go since in the meantime their papa had died and decisions were made by other elders in the family. Eventually permission was given for the trip with a chaperone of course. So Dora and at least one of her sisters, Adelaide I believe, set off on the journey.

Germany at this time was not the great unified country it is today. Instead it was made up of states, principalities and duchies, groupings that came together in federations for protection and mutual interests. Albrecht's home Waldeck and Pyrmont (famous for its spa) was for centuries a royal principality – quite small in size it would later come under the protection of the great state of Prussia. Albrecht's cousin Viktor was the sovereign, a position, which under the right circumstances might be open to Albrecht himself one day – thus the title *His Highness,* which afforded him all the benefits of the royal court including connections to the royals of Britain and the Netherlands.

Shortly after Albrecht's birth in 1841 (probably in Waldeck's Arolsen Castle) in far-off Berlin another birth took place – a baby boy who would grow up to be inevitably linked with Albrecht – Carl Piel.

Carl came from a well-to-do Berlin family and his parents set their sights on getting him placed as a page in the royal household of Waldeck and Pyrmont. This was done by privileged contacts; Carl, though a commoner, was tutored until the age of eleven years when he would then enter the court for grooming in etiquette and service to the royals. Eventually, he would hope to reach a senior position in the royal court or the army. As we shall see Carl would turn out to be no ordinary page.

It was in the year 1851 in the court of Waldeck and Pyrmont that the two boys Albrecht and Carl would have encountered one another for the first time as prince and page. Coming from hundreds of years of royal blood lines Albrecht was distinguished, polite and with a striking presence about him, while Carl had an open, soft-natured and winning way and was confident about everything he undertook. On occasions when the young royals were allowed to fraternise with the pages they would seek one another out for games, swordplay and wandering the castle grounds imagining conquering the world and other great adventures as boys do – a remarkable and inseparable bond was developing between them and with it they were ever popular throughout the court.

They grew up into their teens passing through what the Germans call *Jugendweihe* (coming of age). And all the while they learned to be formal with one another when protocol demanded yet bosom pals when away from their duties. Such bonds have often been seen as selfless giving – the *Good* as the philosopher Aristotle described it – and it led eventually to Carl being appointed as Albrecht's personal manservant. He would treat Carl with absolute respect as he carried out his official duties and be his friend at other times; and for Carl friendship was similar but if need be he would lay down his life for Albrecht – here as we shall see fate had a strange role to play.

Meanwhile, Albrecht's elders were already sounding out marriage possibilities for him with other royal households – the occasion no doubt quickened by the marriage of the prince of a nearby principality to an actress.

It was into all of this in 1864 that Dora Gage arrived in Bonn to be welcomed by Albrecht. Bonn was a considerable journey from Waldeck and Pyrmont so the student prince would be free from the watchful eyes of his court with Carl at his side overseeing everything. So, a full love affair blossomed between Albrecht and Dora.

This brings us to the second and simpler version of our tale. That is that Dora Gage came to Bonn to participate in the lively equestrian scene in the city. Here she met Albrecht; they fell in love and kept it secret, with only Carl knowing until they could find a way of revealing it to the Court of Waldeck and Pyrmont. Not the romantic tale of budding love on the shore of Rathlin Island perhaps, but like the first version at least it places Dora in Bonn with Albrecht in 1864. In very little time the pair decided that even if they were prince and commoner they would marry whatever the cost.

I must add that in all the researches I have ever undertaken, in all the love tales I have ever recounted, once two young people declare their love for one another nothing will pull them apart. Shakespeare said it in *A Midsummer Night's Dream* and for the ancient Romans it was *Amantes amentes – lovers are lunatics* – meaning they are not really crazy but will not let the uncontrollable emotion possessing them be overcome whatever the cost. Nonetheless, Albrecht was well aware that it might shake the court to its foundations. We can imagine then Albrecht turning to his soulmate Carl in desperation, 'What shall I do my good Carl? Must I die of heartbreak…!'

'No you shan't,' would be Carl's reply. 'We shall meet it together. Whatever the cost you must go to your cousin Prince Viktor with the truth and I shall be at your side.'

And that is the way it was, with Victor greatly saddened by Albrecht's declaration of his desire to marry Dora.

'I have no male heir so the sovereignty would be yours if

anything happened to me.' Viktor declared. 'But that cannot now be; you will also forfeit all the favours of the court, nor may you marry within the jurisdiction of Waldeck and Pyrmont. You may however keep the dignity of *Highness* in your title.'

Albrecht had surrendered his rights and such was the gravity of the affair we may well believe he wept on Carl's shoulder.

More was to come for it necessitated what was known as a *Morganatic or Left-handed Marriage*. This ensured the bride had no claims to any of the trappings of royalty her husband might have had. In crude terms it was often a marriage of convenience that was open to abuse. In the late 1700s Frederick of Prussia, said to have many mistresses, also had a *Left-handed Marriage* with one of his favourite ladies while still being in the state of matrimony.

As for the pair's marriage it was decided it would have to take place in Ireland and after much toing and fro-ing it was deemed that the only suitable place for such an unusual ceremony was the chapel of Dublin Castle. Ireland was administered from Dublin Castle so Queen Victoria, having been consulted, gave consent. She also agreed that, commoner or not, a title would have to be conferred on Dora who now would become Dorothea Duchess of Rhoden (a village in Waldeck).

Reports talk of an enormous crowd turning out on Thursday 2 June 1864 to see this unusual wedding. Albrecht wore the dazzling white uniform of a Lieutenant Colonel, with a sword by his side and carrying a plumed gilt helmet, while Dora bedecked in a magnificent gown with a veil of white lace edged in green was accompanied by six bridesmaids – her Gage sisters much to the fore. Then came the strange ceremony with Albrecht extending his *left hand* to the bride to be. One might imagine the surprise if not gasps of the onlookers. Strikingly there were no representatives from Waldeck and Pyrmont. Indeed the only affirmation of the Principality was the presence of the ever loyal Carl who was permitted to stay in the service of Albrecht, now attached to the army.

Albrecht and Dora would go on to have four children, two boys and two girls, the first of these called Robert was born in 1866. It would appear that Dora may not have been in good health afterwards, part of which was homesickness. So, thinking that the presence of one of the Gage sisters would help Dora come to terms with being away from home, it was agreed to send for her sister Adelaide still living in Rathlin Island; thus plans were launched to bring Adelaide to Germany.

Albrecht knew that it would take someone of trust and thorough reliability to convey Adelaide by sea to a port on the northern coast of Germany and thence to Waldeck and Pyrmont. There was only one man for such an important task and so, reluctantly or not, he decided to send Carl – it would be one of few times from childhood that they would be apart and a fateful decision. So, near the end of August 1868 Carl set out for Rathlin Island most likely on the German yacht *Grille*, which was used by royals.

By mid-September to much excitement the elegant *Grille* looking magnificent in full sail anchored in Rathlin Island's Church Bay in full view of the manor house and soon preparations were underway for Adelaide's journey.

Now to the most harrowing part of this story Carl Piel suddenly, unbelievably, died on Rathlin. Here I cannot get Homer's *Illiad* out of my head… '… *Fate? No one alive has ever escaped it, I tell you – it's born with us…*'

There is something of the air of Greek tragedy about our story – the inseparable bond of friendship; the unusual marriage and rejection of royal heritage; the death of the beloved friend. Had we lived in ancient times we might have thought the gods were angry because the predestined path of fate had been interfered with and they took revenge by putting an end to the great friendship between Albrecht and Carl. Others might think it was simply a freakish accident. As it happened Carl Piel was taken ill on Monday 21 September and by the evening of Wednesday 23 sadly he was dead.

So, how did Carl die? Firstly there is little information at all in records about Rathlin Island, excepting a few words that say he died suddenly. Indeed, we only know that he was on the island at all from his tombstone and a plaque in the church. However, after delving deep into many an archive, I have found a clue. Carl Piel most likely died of a bee sting or stings – so my source has revealed. Either he got too close to bee hives in the Gage's garden or suffered a severe allergic reaction from a bee sting when outside. Such a misfortune would have resulted in a quick and unpleasant death.

When the news reached Albrecht one can only guess the heartbreak – neither time nor a thousand royal privileges would repair such a pain. The beautiful bond was broken.

Then the inevitable question – should he have sent Carl in the first place?

Time rolled on. Dora died at the age of 48 and Albrecht at 56. After Dora's death he remarried and moved to the nearby region of Cleve but only lived for nine years.

Interestingly he had another boy whom he christened Carl.

Note: *Being familiar with Rathlin Island (On one occasion I was stormbound there for over a week during a vicious hurricane) I wanted to get at the roots of this tale. This proved difficult for only a throwaway line about it exists locally – one vague story even talks of Albrecht sailing into Rathlin Island and sweeping Dora off her feet. Thus it took much research in archives and newspapers at home and abroad to get to the bottom of it and I trust I've managed to recount the real heart of the affair.*

Carl's family later placed a plaque in German in St. Thomas' Church – it reads:

His brothers and sisters from Berlin and Neustrelitz dedicate this memorial tablet to Carl Piehl, who died here on 24 September 1868, in everlasting memory! (The date given is a day later than on the tombstone and Piel is spelt Piehl.)

The Enagh Aviator – Magnificent Man in his Flying Machine

No bird soars too high if he soars with his own wings
William Blake (1757-1827)

Seagulls soaring over a Donegal shore, a brilliant and inventive mind and a design of world class.

This is the tale of Professor Geoffrey Hill, a man of genius who lived quietly at Enagh Lough near Derry but in his own way transformed the field of aviation right into modern times.

Now for me there is something very special about Enagh Lough – a feeling of the distant past lingers here with the ancient graveyard, the connection with Colmcille and the great O'Cathan castle that once hosted men from the Spanish Armada (1588). Actually, Enagh (from Irish meaning *marshy place*) is really a pair of lakes – East Lake and West Lake, located at the end of Judge's Road, Maydown, in Derry-Londonderry. Antique yes, but my focus on this occasion is something more modern: flight.

Our story really begins with the Wright brothers first powered air flight in 1903. Enthusiasts everywhere started to build gliders and engine driven aeroplanes. Geoffrey was eight years old at the time and it was all the talk in the Hill household in London – his father was a mathematics professor so there was no want of encouragement in building experimental models, and by the time he was a teenager one of Geoffrey's designs was accepted for a schools' exhibition. Just to set the scene locally, Joe Cordner was flying around Derry and Donegal from about 1910 as was Harry Ferguson from County Down and the pair collaborated with flights on Benone Strand.

As for Geoffrey, after university, at twenty-one years of age, having obtained his pilot's licence he very quickly became a test pilot; and with World War I looming he joined the Royal Air Corps, being soon posted to the conflict in France where he was awarded the Military Cross after distinguished service.

He got his first liking for this part of the world in October 1918 when he met and married Mary Alexander, a Tyrone girl whose family owned land at Caw in Waterside and nearby Enagh Lough. It was during their honeymoon at Marble Hill, County Donegal, that Geoffrey had an idea that still very much reverberates in the world of aviation today – tailless aircraft.

Imagine standing on the shore and seeing gulls swing high and soar in swift breezes. This is what he witnessed at Marble Hill and with it came the notion of a single-wing aeroplane without a tail. Seeing the gulls so steady in flight he believed that designing an aircraft based on this idea would solve the problem of destabilisation so apparent in planes of the time. Soon Geoffrey was in demand where planes were being designed and tested. Yet although he was busy night and day he still had time while at the Hanley Page Company to take one of their planes to a world record height of nearly 14,000 feet.

Eventually Geoffrey joined forces with the Westland Company to produce a series of planes he called *Pterodactyls* because of the resemblance to the flying reptiles of Dinosaur times. However, design issues dragged out and eventually the British Air Ministry called a halt to research. Shortly after this he was appointed Professor of Mechanical Engineering at University College London and then with the approach of World War II he was seconded to the Air Ministry to liaise with Canada on aircraft information – recognition of the esteem he was held in.

At the beginning of the 1950s, Geoffrey's and Mary's thoughts turned towards Ireland with plans to settle down at Enagh Lough. The Alexanders, Mary's family, (related in the maternal line to Adam Murray of Derry siege fame), had purchased the lands at Caw and Enagh in the 1600s and Mary's father inherited the house at Enagh in 1874 from his uncle Adam Murray Alexander, barrister-at-law and Judge of the Supreme Court of British Guiana – he gives his name to the local well-known Judge's Road. With her father dying in 1902, and her mother in 1951, Mary and Geoffrey, no strangers to the Enagh house, moved permanently into the dwelling from 1954 and eventually it was inherited by their son Terence Hill.

Curiously enough had Geoffrey been there a decade earlier in 1944 he might well have witnessed the crash of the Royal Navy Fairey Barracuda (DP872) into Enagh Lough with the loss of all three crew. The Barracuda, a design not without its problems, had taken off from nearby *HMS Shriek*, Maydown, and was believed to have stalled before plunging headlong into the lough.

Geoffrey continued to work throughout the early fifties with Short Brothers Belfast on the development of the *Short SB.4 Sherpa* with hope of producing a wingless craft – 'The Sherpa is designed to eliminate distortion so that flying is safer, faster and higher,' said Geoffrey at the time. However, the concept was abandoned before his goal could be realised. Then sadly in 1955 before Geoffrey could promote further aircraft designs he passed away at Enagh where he is buried.

Geoffrey Hill's legacy is enormous – aircraft and models he built are housed in several museums and today's single or flying – wing stealth planes used for reconnaissance high above the earth have benefitted from his designs. He was modest, intellectually brilliant and continuously alert to challenges – something that brought him many friends and many partnerships in aircraft design – in every sense Geoffrey Hill was a true aviation pioneer.

The Mystery of the Unmarked Grave

*Some are born great, some achieve greatness,
and others have greatness thrust upon them*
(William Shakespeare, Twelfth Night)

A few years back wandering through the city cemetery in Derry – Londonderry my attention was taken by an empty plot – a square of grass that stood out simply because there was not the slightest indication why it should be like this in the middle of so many graves. My immediate recourse was to my good friend Pearse Henderson, a man with a keen eye for all things historical and well into knowledge of the City Cemetery's past. Pearse revealed the grave, registered as GC111, was known to him; it was that of a ship's captain, a man who had been declared a hero, who had made it to Derry after an unbelievable survival off the Donegal coast in 1917.

Yet somehow he had been forgotten over the decades – to be precise 105 years. It was simply *the unmarked grave*. What had happened I wondered and why would a hero be laid to rest in such a lonely patch without the slightest recognition?

Soon I discovered that his name was Erik Kokeritz – Captain Erik Kokeritz, Master Mariner, and his story is begging to be told.

Now picture this. It is February 6 1918; the time is almost 2:30 pm in the afternoon and one of the most unusual scenes ever witnessed in Derry is about to unfold. Outside the City Hotel, opposite the Guildhall sits a gun carriage with a coffin draped in the flag of the United States and drawn by four black horses.

To the great shock of everyone, the rescued Captain Kokeritz has died suddenly and is about to be laid to rest with a tribute the likes of which have never been seen.

Crowds gather for the funeral, for folk have taken him to their hearts. At the front of the procession are bands and servicemen, then officials – representatives of America, Sweden and the home countries; then city fathers, clergy, men from the local Sailors' Rest and finally vast numbers of the public.

The weather marks the mood of the occasion, grey, cold and snowy – grim and sombre. The horrible carnage of World War I lingers in every nook and cranny.

With a wave of the chief bandmaster's baton at 2:30 precisely, the bands strike up the *Dead March from Saul* and the procession moves off with mechanical precision towards the city cemetery.

Only weeks ago excitement swept through Derry with the news that Captain Kokeritz and twenty-two of his crew had been rescued from their open lifeboat off the entrance to Lough Swilly after their ship the *SS Rochester* had been torpedoed by a German U Boat some 400 miles off the Irish coast. They had drifted for five days and five nights in hazardous gales and extreme cold, the men determined to stay alive thanks to the encouragement and fortitude of their captain who had remained awake most of the time to keep them safe.

What was the background of this remarkable man?

Erik Kokeritz, Swedish by birth, was born in May 1874 and brought up in the ancient fishing port of Gavle on Sweden's Eastern seaboard, about 170 kilometres from the capital Stockholm. Erik's boyhood dream was to get to sea. America was the main attraction at the time so in 1894 at the age of twenty he took the opportunity to take passage to Australia with the hope of travelling on from there to San Francisco where he would meet up with his sister Ingrid.

Emigrants wanted to become naturalised Americans and now based in San Francisco, Erik achieved this after a number of unsuccessful attempts. He also commenced to get seafaring experience on trading vessels and by 1910 at the age of thirty-six was in line for his captain's ticket and charge of his own vessel.

Soon he was being recognised as a solid and reliable captain.

Setting the scene at this time World War I had commenced in 1914 but America did not join Britain in the fight against Germany. However, like it or not American shipping trade was affected, since Kaiser Wilhelm had placed a no shipping or War Zone around Ireland, Britain, and the western coast of France. This meant a hazardous voyage for any vessels prepared to run the gauntlet of dozens of patrolling U-boats armed with deadly torpedoes. As a consequence a system of naval convoy escorts in and out of the North West approaches to Ireland and Britain offered some protection. Yet the risk to vessels was still considerable and nothing at all was available for France now cut off completely from incoming supplies from the West.

America and Germany were living uncomfortably with one another and immense strain was put on the relationship with the sinking of the *RMS Lusitania* off Cork in May 1915, when 1,198 souls were lost 128 of whom were Americans. Frustration was growing in the States that vessels were unable to do business with France and eventually after consulting the government two American shipping lines declared they would break the submarine blockade and enter the southern port of Bordeaux in France. The companies were the Kerr Steamship Line and the Oriental Navigation Company. They would ignore German restrictions but would have American flags painted on their sides.

After much toing and fro-ing, Kerrs chose Captain Kokeritz for their vessel the *SS Rochester* while Oriental opted for Captain Tucker for the *SS Orleans* – Kokeritz was 43 years old and Tucker almost ten years younger. Both vessels were just short of 3000 tons and would carry cargoes of wheat, canned food, cotton, medical supplies, machinery and clothes. The duration of the trip would be about fourteen days.

As the ships prepared for departure on 10 February 1917, excitement was mounting throughout America about the outcome of the venture. Many folk were viewing it as a race between the two captains to see who would reach Bordeaux first but in France it was more a case of seeing if the War Zone could be broken.

The Germans saw it as a trip of folly.

Thinking about the two captains it seems to me that contrasting personalities were to the fore. My impression is that Tucker was more cavalier, a man who saw adventure in it, while Kokeritz viewed it more purposefully. Both were determined but there is a sense of less show with Kokeritz, a feeling of 'Let's get the job done'.

In the end Tucker was first into Bordeaux, the date being 27 February 1917 and Kokeritz arrived three days later on 2 March. Such was the joy of seeing the ships that competition was forgotten – thousands turned out to greet them, there were celebrations, banquets and presentations given by the leading citizens of Bordeaux and both were presented with medals to mark the occasion. Then on 12 March Kokeritz and Tucker were summoned to Paris to meet the French government and once again they were wined and dined and presented with medals and citations. It was as if the war had been won and in the end a considerable slap in the face for Germany.

As to be expected, the German hierarchy played down the triumph of Tucker and Kokeritz but it is difficult to believe they would not have been in a position to torpedo the vessels had they wished. One can only assume that they wanted to avoid increasing the already tense situation with America especially after the recent sinking of the British vessel the *RMS Laconia* on 25 February when American lives were lost again. Nonetheless the Kaiser placed a bounty of $10,000 on the heads of Kokeritz and Tucker and further increased the threat to any shipping American or otherwise.

The American government reacted and from this time onwards American trading ships had mounted guns and operating crews as an extra precaution.

It is at this juncture that we leave Tucker to have many more exploits though we shall hear of him later in our story. For now the light shines on Kokeritz and the path to greatness for the man whose final days were spent in Derry-Londonderry. This I suppose is the way destiny works for the bravery of breaking the blockade of France turns out to be merely a step on his way to the dizzy heights of being a national hero.

On 15 August, 1917, Captain Kokeritz was asked to take *SS Rochester* from Baltimore to Manchester with a full cargo, which he did successfully and then set out on the return trip to America. On Thursday 1 November, *Rochester* entered the North West approaches with other vessels on convoy but the following day instead of going South (with the convoy) Kokeritz opted to go directly due West across the ocean to Baltimore.

It proved to be a fateful decision, as we enter the live action.

Firstly signs of danger. Earlier in the day the watch reports seeing a periscope. Then just about supper time comes that which all fear – out of nowhere with a mighty blast a torpedo lifts the vessel right out of the water. She is hit mid-ships, the engine room and all vital services destroyed.

Captain Kokeritz cries, 'They got us!'

As to be expected there is chaos, fire, and billowing smoke and men running everywhere, the damage unrepairable and shouts for the three lifeboats to be lowered.

Meanwhile, the submarine that fired the torpedo surfaces and callously continues to shell the *Rochester* – such acts, the evils of war, the things that men do on their fellow men.

Seafarers will tell you that there is a bond between them, the sea, and their ship – lying in their bunks at night they are familiar with every creak, every pitch and yaw, every mood of the wind and the waves. They are comrades together, the vessel is their home, the captain their leader. I am reminded of the words of Richard Dana in *Two Years Before the Mast*:

A dozen men are shut up together in a little bark upon the wide,

wide sea, and for months and months see no forms and hear no voices but their own, and when one is taken suddenly from among them they miss him at every turn...

Everything aboard the *SS Rochester* has been shattered but *cometh the hour cometh the man*; immediately Captain Kokeritz is everywhere, directing, helping and encouraging – urging his men into the lifeboats and ignoring his own safety collecting anything that will be useful for their survival. The three lifeboats huddle together bumping into the side of the vessel, the men calling for the captain to join them and at last he does. There are twenty-two in his lifeboat, the Chief Mate has thirteen and the Second Mate twelve.

Then the saddest thing one might imagine. The lifeboats start to drift apart on the churning sea – there are attempts at shaking hands, shouts of good luck and farewell and suddenly all three boats are in the lap of the gods. Soon they will be aware of that saying of old seadogs when disaster strikes, 'Shift for yourselves!' The only blessings are that the weather is calm and coming on to darkness the Germans will not spot them. But, they are at least 400 miles from the nearest landfall – Ireland.

We stay with Captain Kokeritz's lifeboat, noting that eventually after a horrendous journey the second lifeboat under the Chief Mate makes it to Portacloy on the coast of County Mayo in Ireland. Of the thirteen originally on this boat nine die, four of whom are buried locally at Kilgalligan Cemetery. Nothing is ever heard again of the third lifeboat.

Taking the tiller of his boat Kokeritz organises a schedule of rowing, eating, water allowance and resting. A stiff South West wind gives them steady progress under sail for two days and nights but the cramped conditions with the twenty-two souls packed like sardines makes moving and general hygiene absolutely ghastly and only the captain's continual inspiration maintains the men's morale.

After two days the wind strengthens towards hurricane force; all hands are getting soaked with the icy sea breaking over the boat and with waves reaching thirty feet at times Kokeritz orders the sail to be lowered. They manage to further stabilise the craft with temporary anchors over the sides. These large canvas bags full of water do their job but unfortunately after a time they are ripped away and only the oars save the day.

The more North they drift the more the temperature drops so that legs become frozen and most begin suffering from frostbite. 'Stay with us men!' Urges the captain who, locking the tiller, moves among them lifting their spirits. There is no doubt it is needed for fatigue is setting in – despair more evident by the hour.

But then a glimmer of hope on the 8 November. Far to the East there is a faint flash of light.

Cries of joy go up. 'It's Tory – Tory Light!'

Tory Island lies a few miles off the Irish coast and houses the first beacon of light for incoming vessels to Derry.

Kokeritz leaps into action steering a few points North as the dark outline of land appears. It is an unforgiving rocky coastline that immediately calls for his exhausted oarsmen to keep a steady tack away from the shore.

It is the fifth day and night of their ordeal.

Time passes and the following day miraculously – seemingly out of nowhere, they spot an off-shore patrol boat in the distance. Immediately they wave and shout frantically. Heaven sent it is, for the patrol boat has also seen them; in little time it is alongside their battered craft and within minutes, barely able to walk, they are lifted to safety.

At this stage they are at the entrance to Lough Swilly. However, the nearest hospital where they can get treatment for frostbite and exposure is in Derry. So the patrol boat makes for the little port of Buncrana on Lough Swilly about fifteen miles from the city. Within a couple of hours the twenty-two crewmen are being checked at the Derry infirmary; those most badly affected – about half the complement are kept in the hospital – while the rest are taken to the local Sailors' Rest.

Imagine the excitement when it is discovered that Captain Kokeritz, the man who broke the German War Zone, is the men's saviour.

Yet worryingly the captain is adjudged to have threatening pneumonia and the owner of the City Hotel offers him a room and all their facilities. Yet he is not well and after another medical examination is advised to take to his bed. This he does for some days but the pressure from well-wishers and responses to officials do little for his condition. Added to this, townsfolk want to know more about their miraculous survival. Up and about again he is greeted as a hero and spends his time between visiting his men in the hospital and the Sailors' Rest.

The weeks drift into January 1918, Christmas being low key with the grim details from the War the only bright news is that America has joined Britain in the fight against Germany.

Meanwhile, some of Kokeritz's men are well enough to travel back to the States and on 4 February the captain himself looks in on the Guildhall at a concert to raise money for the war effort. Yet folk remark that he is very ill and on returning to the hotel his host sends immediately for the doctor. Rampant pneumonia with complications has set in and sadly that evening to the shock and utter grief of everyone Captain Eric Kokeritz passes away.

Thus was the great gathering on 6 February 1918 for the funeral of the man who achieved greatness while caring for the safety of others and had broken the German blockade – a true hero.

Yet there is a happy ending. On my trip to the vacant plot in the cemetery I was joined by a research colleague David Jenkins. David was seized by the idea that the captain should be recognised and as a result gathered every fragment of information about him and his bravery. The outcome is a book *Captain Kokeritz,* a video, a beautiful gravestone in Derry cemetery and dedication ceremonies both in the city and at Kilgalligan in County Mayo where a gravestone has also been erected.

Remarkably the once vacant plot is now occupied with a

Never Forgotten

The Magical Hats of Madame Beck

Without hats there is no civilization
(Christian Dior)

On a bitter October day in 1939 a group of 20 men and women wrapped up from the cold, stepped off the Belfast train in Derry's Waterside station with what can only be called the most basic of luggage. Believe it or not these folk were Jews who virtually overnight had fled Vienna in Austria and by a circuitous often perilous route had eventually made it to here.

To say they were nervous and perplexed would certainly not be an over-statement. Here they were in Northern Ireland a strange land and to further complicate their plight a strange language to deal with – most having only a smattering of English.

It was once said, 'When you're fleeing for your life, don't pause to grab the family silver.'

Nothing was truer for these folk who were more or less penniless.

Already thousands of Jews across Europe were being terrorised, many were transported to concentration camps and many were put to death.

Within a month, March to be precise, Hitler invaded Vienna in what has come to be known as the *Anschluss*.

As you might expect this group of Jews on the platform were in shock. The contrast could not have been greater – Vienna – world renowned city – romance, Mozart and Beethoven , great writers and artists, breath-taking palaces and of course the *Blue Danube* – Derry so different; an old-world historic town set in exquisite scenery but on the edge of war having been chosen as the hub for the defence of the Northern Atlantic . There were air raid shelters in every street, guard houses on main thoroughfares, anti-aircraft guns on the roofs of high buildings and barrage balloons high up in the sky – the city would soon be teeming with young service folk from all over the world with warships five abreast on the River Foyle and three air bases nearby.

There was however something special waiting for these visitors, an X-factor soon to be apparent – a Derry welcome, an Irish welcome – as the world and his neighbour knows a place where the hand of friendship reaches out to one and all. Suddenly, as if out of nowhere our little group is surrounded by fathers of the city, clergy, business folk, well-wishers, and believe it or not some local Jews for Derry had its own congregation from 1900 – names such as Szilagy, Lazarus, Pollock, Spain, Frieslander and Shenkel no strangers in the locality.

The task now was to make this new group feel at home in the city – a welcome meal, accommodation and then discuss what occupations they could take up. Many would be skilled in top professions so it might take time to find appropriate work. Happily there would be employment – one even having the offer of horse breeding.

A most unusual pursuit was that chosen by Madame Georgette Beck who, ably assisted by her husband Ernst, decided on millinery. Georgette and Ernst were allotted lodgings in the North of the city at Pennyburn with the promise of their own apartment at the Farm, a large house close by, which had originally been the home of the Londonderry MP Sir Robert Ferguson. Folk remembered their accommodation as pleasant with French fashion magazines and French music from artistes such as Maurice Chavalier and Jean Sablon.

In little time everyone was talking about Madame Beck and Ernst – but why millinery?

It turned out that she was highly skilled in the making of hats indeed had been involved in the haut-couture of hat making; now with the assistance of Ernst she would set up a millinery business – making fancy ladies' hats – the like of it had never been heard of in Derry so the city was awash with expectation.

Yet who was Madame Beck and, Vienna apart, where exactly had she come from?

Georgette Beck was born of wealthy parents in Paris in 1899 most likely in the Marais – a Jewish quarter. Her father who was not a Jew was descended from a very old European family, while her mother who was Jewish was of the Low-Beer dynasty – industrialists and leaders in wool and sugar production. Both families were Czech with close ties to Vienna. Georgette, who had two sisters, was highly educated and introduced to haut-couture millinery in Paris. Then through family contacts she opened a millinery shop in Vienna in the 1930s and there met and married a German Jew, Ernst Beck. By doing so her nationality changed from French to German as was the law at the time. Ernst now began helping her with her hat making business. This consisted of a fashionable shop and show room where her amazing hats were on display, all of them made in an adjoining studio.

We can imagine the women of Vienna – princesses, duchesses and visiting ladies from all across Europe flocking to marvel at the wonderful creations in *Boutique Georgette*. Cleverly she would use seductive titles such as – *Destiny, Starlight and Mystique* to charm her clientele – the shop an *Aladdin's Cave* of delight for hat lovers, her studio a place of wonder for those allowed a glance – bales of silk, satin, felt and expensive cloth, ribbons and feathers of every hue and shelf after shelf of mannequin heads with hats in every stage of completion – a hive of industry with half a dozen girls sewing and tirelessly cutting and shaping under the watchful eye of the intrepid Madame Beck.

All of this the Nazis wiped out with their invasion of Vienna that sent Jewish folk fleeing across Europe.

Madame Beck was reaching 40 years of age when she arrived in Derry. She was slim, tall, with a classical oval face and very assured, her French accent still much to the fore.

Her idea was that a woman was not complete without a hat, the style really down to how she and her clients agreed on what suited. This then was why women so much enjoyed the experience of visiting her Viennese shop and this was the talent that had suddenly arrived in Derry.

After being introduced to the local business scene she and Ernst set about planning the opening of their millinery shop. However, given the scarcities of war she would never be able to match the scale of her earlier venture. Nonetheless, they found very suitable premises in the heart of the city in Sackville Street, an old-fashioned and attractive thoroughfare. Her friendly and outward personality made it easy to deal with people and soon she had enough basic materials to launch her new venture with a simple sign saying:

Madame Beck, Milliner

Modest it might have been but when her first creations saw the light of day in Derry it was a sensation – 'Magical!' it was said.

She had produced special designs the like of which would usually only be seen in the great stores of London, Paris and New York. Meanwhile, Madame Beck had joined groups such as the Womans' Institute and the Londonderry Soroptimist's Club. Also, working for the war effort, on one occasion at a fair for raising funds she delighted everybody by dressing up as a fortune teller, her French accent adding to the fun of it all.

Well embedded in the community Georgette and Ernst became British citizens in 1948.

Then with World War II well behind her in 1953, she felt it was time to expand her millinery business. Her thoughts turned to Vienna and all the paraphernalia of hat making that she had left behind in her shop. It would be just the thing if she could reclaim it. So, she started out on the long haul back to Austria and to a Vienna just shaking itself free from the dark days of war. Yet upon arrival, joy and disappointment – her shop was still there, still operating but the occupiers would not give up her hat making tools or materials. It took a struggle and a longer stay than she intended for she had to have recourse to the law. It fell within the ambit of post-war reconciliation tribunals and to her delight she was awarded all her possessions. Some weeks later the *SS Fairhead* of the Ulster Steamship Co. sailed into Derry with everything in tact – it was a triumph. After that the business flourished not just in Derry but beyond with day-to-day hats and special occasion hats – weddings a speciality. At one stage records show that she had eight girls working for her.

Husband Ernst was always in the background encouraging and supporting the more flamboyant Georgette as he had originally done in Vienna. They had no family but they took advantage of the offer of a white Scottie dog – this their pride and joy as they moved into their sixties and were now well accepted as an integral part of the Derry community.

Ernst was a small, quiet, genial man, always mindful of the loss of his family to the Nazis but he and Georgette had taken Ireland to their hearts and no way would they ever consider leaving. He set up a leather wallet making business but became ill in 1963 and after a difficult period in Altnagelvin Hospital to the heartbreak of Georgette he passed way – the final chapter in their loving 40-year marriage.

It was the beginning of the end for Derry's high class hat business. Georgette slipped away and with money believed to have been left to her in Ernst's Will built a bungalow for herself at Fahan, County Donegal. Her twilight years by the sea in the 70s and 80s were peaceful and well earned. In time Madame Georgette Beck became frail and went under the care of the nuns at the Nazareth House in Fahan passing away at the grand old age of 89 years.

She was laid to rest at St. Mura's Church of Ireland, Fahan.

Note: *The Low-Beer family on Madame Beck's maternal side are associated with Schlinder's List having owned the factory that Oskar Schlinder used to provide occupation and sustenance for Jewish folk.*

Lyster's Golden Touch

I like to be on time!
(Lyster Jackson on his clocks)

If there is a hall of fame for Derry characters of the past it must surely include Lyster Jackson. By the way, it is Lyster not Lester, his Christian name coming from an earlier branch of the family and his full name being – Henry Lyster Douglas Jackson.

He was born into a time in the early 1900s when aspiring amateur engineers turned their hands to combustion engines, aeroplanes, machines, building and repairing – indeed just about everything. In all of these Lyster had the so called *Golden Touch* – he was successful at anything he turned his hand to. Of course there were many like him but for sheer variety and audacity with it I put him high up on the list – if you built a spanking new wooden hulled yacht, Lyster would counter it saying – 'Yes, I did that too and now come and see my new shining one made of metal!'

He was ahead of the pack in anything to do with engines, fabrication, indeed all things mechanical – throw in a champion at chess, sailing, repairs of all sorts and the list goes on. Although his name is now forgotten in researching Derry's past I come across it frequently not just because of his talent but also because of his nature and ebullience.

As it happened I first encountered Lyster in an 'inside – out', or perhaps I should say, 'upside-down' way for I heard of him before I ever knew his name or what he was about. My mother, who attended every evening class under the sun from cake baking to flower arranging and heaven knows what, returned home one evening from a carpentry session to say her whole class had been astonished by the magnificent French polishing work that one of the students had brought in to show them. She did not know his name and while I didn't attach too much to it, in the curious twisting path that life is, I was to come across this same man years later – it was Lyster Jackson and as you'll hear he had a surprise in store for me.

So who was Lyster Jackson? I want to take you back about a hundred years or so to the Springtown area of Derry. At this stage this spot is in the country and the local big house is called Ballinaska or Springtown House. Herein live the Jacksons a well-heeled family – father Harry is the local manager of the Belfast Steamship Company, mother Annie is a Dublin girl very refined, educated abroad. Both are highly valued in the community, both are ardent church goers at Christ Church, C of I, Infirmary Road, Londonderry. By the end of the first decade of the 1900s they have three children, two boys and a girl – Lyster the youngest is about nine years of age. They have a cook, a servant, a governess and a gardener.

Newspaper reports talk of the beautiful garden and orchard at Springtown House the pride and joy of Annie the children's mother; and from a postcard I've been lucky to find dated 1908 there appears to have been a special bond between Annie and Lyster – the card, from Dublin, has a picture of two playful cats on a wall and reads:

'Master Lyster Jackson, Ballinska, Springtown Road, Lononderry.

Back tomorrow, GNR Station, at 3:15 p.m. and hope to see you. I was very glad to get your postcard – Mother.'

Lyster was coming to seven years of age at that time.

In 1911 Lyster's father died suddenly yet it would be 36 years later in 1947 before his mother would pass away – having resided in Dublin with her daughter before her death. Lyster lived at Springtown House before and after his mother's passing and upon reaching school leaving age had got employment in the repair of motor vehicles – quite a prestigious occupation in those early days. By the way, Derry got its first registered automobile in 1911, a Model T Ford owned by M.A. Robinson the city engineer.

As for Lyster, from the 1920s onwards we can begin to build up a picture of the man who was to become almost a household name in the North West. Reports show that he was the 'go to man' for difficult jobs and delicate fabrication work. He had the 'Golden Touch' one might say and as a pastime he built his own car, designed the body work and labelled it prominently as:

The Lyster Jackson

The more I poured over reports and past newspapers the more I got the picture of someone not just with flair and talent in engineering but also a man with an amazing range of pursuits. Alongside all of this a remarkable personality was developing. He became more assured and outward; as the saying goes Lyster was not backward in coming forward and in truth he became just as well known for his temperament as he was for his 'hands on' capabilities.

In some ways he had become larger than life and some might say not a little eccentric. In appearance he was of average height, with wavy hair, good features and very expressive eyes. I get the impression from folk who knew him that he would not suffer fools gladly and there was a compulsive side to him as is evidenced when he caught a young boy up one of his apple trees pocketing some of the fruit – it was not a case of 'Don't ever let me catch you doing this again!' Instead Lyster had the boy fined ten shillings – a mighty sum imposed on a child in those days and I wonder was it really necessary.

However it tells us that he took no prisoners – without doubt something that fuelled his competitive spirit. No surprise then that chess suited him. His agile mind made him very welcome in chess circles and he could hold his own against great Ulster champions such as Derry man Eugene O'Hare, one of the outstanding players in the country.

Being Lyster he did not stop at this for we next find him among the winners in yacht racing at Lough Swilly. It seems on one occasion he stunned club members when he arrived with a steel-hulled yacht complete with aluminium mast – it was so unusual it made headlines in the local newspapers.

By the 1940s Lyster had married Dilys – a wonderful match and sealing the union they had a son in 1945. In a way it sort of 'seasoned' his existence and made him more settled as one might say. He often referred to Dilys as 'Lady Jackson'.

Then, as mid-life approached Lyster left Springtown house and moved to a smaller residence about a couple of miles away. Though still active in the 1950s and 60s, come the 1970s as he slowed down, he became very interested in finer furniture and clock mechanics.

It was at this juncture that our paths crossed and I must confess that I knew absolutely nothing about Lyster or his talents before this.

It happened that the BBC offered me some presenting work in the late 70s and I set about doing a radio piece on *Time* – a radio programme about folk whose lives were governed by time; folk who collected timepieces or in one way or another worked in the various dimensions of time. At this stage a friend asked did I know Lyster Jackson to which I answered no. 'He builds and finishes clocks stunningly,' came the reply, 'I'll ask if he'll speak with you.'

Days later the outcome was my knock on his door, which was opened straightaway and there was Lyster Jackson – 'I was expecting you,' said he with a smile, 'do come in.'

Having explained what I was after he felt we could best speak in a back room in a place that to say the least was very dark. Anyway, having switched on my recorder we chatted in what was a really nice interview about how he had turned to clock making. All the while my eyes were adjusting to the darkness and gradually I began to see what looked like long dark cases or coffins – six of them against the walls. What on earth I thought as Lyster rambled on and I began to feel distinctly uncomfortable.

Then, suddenly, several muffled mechanical clicks and would you believe the loudest chimes you have ever heard rang out from six grandfather clocks – not coffins! You could have knocked me over with a feather – in fact I jumped off my chair as Lyster roaring with laughter leaned over, eyes popping, and looking me straight in the face exclaimed – 'You see young man I like to be on time!'

When he put the light on what I saw were six beautiful French polished grandfather clocks – indeed works of art. I think the idea was that strong sunlight can be damaging thus the darkened room.

I am pleased to say the radio piece worked really well – helped by Lyster, but sad to relate about a year later in October 1980 Lyster Jackson aged 78 years and one of Derry's last great characters passed away.

A light had indeed gone out.

Note: *As a point of interest, the great Knox coach that tradition associates with the killing of Mary Ann Knox is now in Derry's Tower Museum. However, originally it was on view in the City Museum in Gwyn's Institution, Brook Park; then, when the museum was closed it went missing. It is reputed to have been discovered badly broken up under a pile of hay in the barn at Ballinskea House (Springtown House).*

I have often wondered how it got there. Perhaps Lyster thought he might restore it?

The Watts and the *Whiskey Man*

When Aeneas Coffey stepped off the Dublin coach in Derry's Diamond in early spring 1833 Andrew Alexander Watt and his son David were there to greet him. Alexander Watt was in partnership with Ross Smyth in a distillery in Abbey Street built on the site of an old monastery; the output was modest but the Watts were a go-ahead family and their true aim was to build a whiskey empire.

Coffey had invented a new still for the production of whiskey and it was quite a coup to get him to come to Derry. The title the *Whiskey Man* was well earned for there was nothing he did not know about whiskey distilling. He had started as a gauger and come up through the ranks to be Chief Inspector for the Excise before retiring. Yet this was not his first visit to the North West for as a young inspector he had waged war against the poteen makers of Inishowen and came off the worst for it.

Inishowen was known as the *Poteen Kingdom* with as many as 800 illicit stills and a trade that reached as far as Scotland. It was boasted that a bottle of poteen could be bought on street corners in Derry for a couple of pence – a brew much better than the official government whiskey.

Over dinner Coffey told the Watts – 'When I was here as a young man I was attacked by about 50 men near Culdaff – they fractured my skull and gave me two bayonet wounds, one of which perforated my thigh…do you know to this day I feel the bad effects of it…'

Yet all his experiences came together in the design of his new still. It would avoid the cumbersome 'batching' in the pot still process so output would be vastly improved. Pot stills were large copper bulbous vessels, while Coffey's method involved steel or copper vertical columns where steam could rise through fermented wash before condensing.

'I've designed a continuous process – the Patent Still I call it,' Coffey went on.

The Watts had their ears to the ground and were always hard-headed in business so they were quick to say – 'But we've heard the big distilleries in the South have turned you down.'

'Let them wear the dunce's hat! I'm bringing you a lifetime's experience,' Coffey retorted.

'And wasn't there a question of taste – lacks tongue?' the Watts further probed.

'Blending will remedy that,' Coffey answered. 'I'll stand by it.'

So the discussion went on. Yet before that evening was out, Watts agreed to take the Coffey Still and urged him to stay on in Derry to work on the making and installing of his invention – the lure an option on another.

It was the first such commercial still in Ireland and typical of the Watt's foresight in business. Now they could put their plan into action but it would be gradual. They would buy out Ross Smyth, put David Watt in charge and secure the eight acres of land from the bottom of Creggan Hill down to Bogside. Large warehouses would be built for whiskey maturing in barrels and sheds the size of football pitches constructed for spreading the dampened grain before fermentation in vats (tuns) of up to 50,000 gallons; this for preparing the mash before condensation in the still.

Coffey moved on to Scotland while, in Derry, the Watts complex was becoming as big as a small town. They were fortunate to have a good supply of water, grains from local famers, and a very good workforce; nearby was a flourishing Derry port for export to all over the world especially America.

In Scotland Coffey's invention was taken up by at least 20 distilleries – his name securing a place on the roll of honour for bringing success to the *Scotch Whisky* industry.

Watts were soon up to an output of over a million gallons a year and were now major players in the economy of Derry and the wider North West. As David Watt neared retiring age A.A. Watt Jnr. who was being groomed to take over stepped in to take the reins. A.A. was a flinty no nonsense character – dapper in appearance and with a lifestyle of military precision no one dared cross him. Driving the local operation to its maximum he drew the Belfast distilleries into the Watt's fold so that output rose to 6,000,000 million gallons a year. The main brands were The Favourite, Inishowen and the Tyrconnell. It was said that Inishowen was titled so as to be in opposition to the poteen trade while the Tyrconnell was called after their novice horse that won at 100-1 in a race in Dublin.

With business flourishing A.A. Jnr. eyed the Scottish producers his aim seemingly to take over the whole of the Scottish industry. Yet the Scottish Distillers would not be outdone and secured a deal in shares that effectively left him cornered. Then in trying secretly to get round the deal he lost the trust of the Scottish Distillers and came out of it badly.

It was to be the beginning of the end for Watts with A.A. Jnr. suffering a series of setbacks early in the 1900s. Firstly, a fire in the Abbey Street Distillery in 1915 caused all the storage vats to be opened so that whiskey flowed down the gutters and crowds flocked to the site to get bucket-fulls of the precious liquid. Next came the 'Green Tax' preventing the sale of newly made whiskey for three years and then the final blow with Prohibition threatened in America – a main outlet.

In 1921with poor times in Derry the workers demanded more money but A.A. Jnr. refused so that a confrontation developed with the workers blocking the Abbey Street entrance to the distillery. A.A. Jnr. arrived in his yellow Rolls Royce one frosty morning demanding he be allowed to enter but was refused. Climbing up on one of his whiskey barrels he cried – 'Well men, shall you open the gates?' to which the reply came, not until their pay was raised. 'Very well,' said Watt, 'shut they are and shut they shall remain.' With these belligerent words A.A. Jnr. put an end to Watt's Distillery and left Derry with one of the darkest days in its colourful history. Up to 300 workers lost their jobs including blenders, coopers, plumbers, general workers and ancillary staff, not to mention the loss to farmers and general suppliers. Alongside this a flourishing pig industry that had built up through a by-product from the distillery called 'pottle' was ruined.

A.A. Watt Jnr. retired to England and dying in 1928 left £900,000 – millions in today's money. It took until 1925 to clear out the Abbey Street distillery and close the operation officially. However, there were vats of whiskey and many barrels of whiskey to be disposed of. This was dealt with by a holding company called Iriscot that continued to trade until 1972.

The last vestige of Watts in Derry is the large warehouse building at Distillery Brae in Waterside – part of the Waterside Distillery that closed along with Abbey Street in 1921. The Waterside distillery at 50 Spencer Road was a significant loss; the Watts had kept the old copper pot stills there and with a process of several distillations made a pot still single malt whiskey that was one of their finest.

As for Aeneas Coffey, the *Whiskey Man,* he established the firm of Aeneas Coffey & Sons in Dublin, but, apart from Watts, the continued lack of interest of the big Irish distillers to adopt his still caused him to move to The Tower Hamlets district of London in 1839. Nearby, in Bow, the firm John Dore & Co adopted his processes and though now in Guilford to this day they continue to make apparatus based on the Coffey principle.

Aeneas died on 1 December 1852 aged 72 years; yet while buried in obscurity in Tower Hamlets he had left the world of whisky an unparalleled legacy.

Although the Watts had cast a shadow over Derry unwittingly they placed Aeneas Coffey in the whiskey hall of fame.

Note: *In Ireland and America 'Whiskey' is used for the spelling while in Scotland and elsewhere 'Whisky' is used.*

Andrew Watt Jnr, is dealt with in Volume I of Ken McCormack's Derry and the Mystery Of Florinda Watt, A.A. Jnr's. aunt, who died in Rome in 1897, is still being researched.(see Volume II)

The Watts originally came from Scotland in the early 1600s and lived at Claragh, Ramelton, Co. Donegal. One of the family Samuel went to Jamaica, where he operated a plantation with slaves – this part of the rum making trade. It is likely that rum sent back by him to Ireland was available when the Watts first opened a store at 7-9 Bishop Street, Derry – this eventually led to the great Watts whiskey empire.

The Killing of Lord Leitrim

*'In this plain oak coffin is the body of Lord Leitrim;
so hated was he that . . . before being placed here the
mob tried to throw his remains into the Liffey…'*
(Verger in the crypt of St Michan's Church, Dublin)

In the first few weeks of the opening of BBC Radio Foyle in 1979 I suggested to Station Manager Ian Kennedy and News Editor Kieran Gill that I would like to do a documentary on the killing of Lord Leitrim(the 3rd Earl of Leitrim) – a sinister incident that occurred over tenant land rights in Fanad, Co. Donegal in 1878. My suggestion was greeted with enthusiasm and here I must say that Ian and Kieran are among the top professionals and mentors I have ever worked with.

The intrigue of the story was that the assassins of Lord Leitrim were known but never named at the time and never convicted; also the circumstances surrounding the issue were as alive in 1979 as they were at the time of the killing. Indeed I was told by friends in Donegal that I would have to exercise the greatest sensitivity if I travelled to Fanad to investigate the Leitrim affair.

A further attraction was that the investigation into the killing in 1878 gave rise to one of the first detective-type stories in Ireland – the first ever tale of this genre being *Murders in the Rue Morgue* by Edgar Allan Poe in 1841.

On becoming the 3rd Earl Lord Leitrim had inherited 92,000 acres of land and had embarked on reforming his estates, a move that put many of his tenants against him especially in the Fanad area of Donegal where evictions were carried out ruthlessly. His argument was that the manner of reforms was his business and that tenants could not do as they pleased. Lord Leitrim's character was resolute and unwavering; from boyhood he had a quick tempered nature yet at times he could be quite generous and even affable. However, at Fanad affairs had gone beyond any compromise.

Fanad Penninsula has some of Ireland's most beautiful scenery. Lough Swilly lies to the east and going west one finds the town of Milford and the road to the town of Carrigart that sits between Mulroy Bay and Sheephaven Bay. It was along this route on 2 April 1878 that Lord Leitrim planned to travel from his home at Manor Vaughan, outside Carrigart, via Milford and on to Derry.

Detailed accounts of the anger brewing note that there were failed attempts on the life of Lord Leitrim, after which at a meeting in a barn in Fanad three men were chosen to carry out his assassination once and for all. According to authors Liam Dolan and Dr.Leslie Lucas, the three men were Neil Shiels of Doughmore, an itinerant tailor, Michael Hergarty of Tullyconnell, and Michael McElwee of Ballyworiskey; others were party to the scheme. The spot chosen for the killing was Cratlagh Wood about three miles from Milford.

Early on the morning of 2 April 1878 Lord Leitrim set out from Manor Vaughn, his party comprising himself, clerk John Makim, and coachman Charles Buchanan and in a second conveyance were his valet William Kincaid and Michael Logue, the driver.

At a spot where the road dipped at Cratlagh Wood the assassins lay in wait and as Lord Leitrim's coach slowed on the upward slope their shots rang out shattering the morning stillness. Charles Buchanan was struck and died immediately; then John Makim fell mortally wounded. Lord Leitrim sustained wounds to his shoulder but jumped from the coach and was wrestling with one of the assailants when, as later revealed, the third brought a red gunstock down on his head with a crack and killed him outright. Bizarrely, Lord Leitrim was still clutching the beard of the assailant who had to be cut free, leaving a tuft of ginger hair still clasped in the dead earl's hand.

It was reported afterwards that one of the assailants had left the scene before the attack and that after the shooting the other two had rowed away across Mulroy Bay in the direction of Fanad.

Folk rushed to the assassination spot and eventually the three bodies were taken to Milford. Meanwhile, word of the killings had been sent to County Inspector Peter Carr who travelled to Milford to inspect the bodies and then moved on to the scene of the shootings. Here he was given guns that had been left behind, also a red gunstock, and significantly a crumpled piece of paper that when straightened turned out to be a page from a child's school copybook.

Having an ear to the ground it was not long before the constabulary turned their attentions to Fanad; houses of vocal protestors about Lord Leitrim were searched and arrests were made. Meanwhile a coroner's court determined that:

The deceased Lord Leitrim and Charles Buchanan came by their deaths by wounds inflicted by persons unknown…and that the deceased John Makim died of an effusion of blood to the brain again perpetrated by persons unknown…

Following this at a pre-trial hearing it was determined beyond doubt that the owner of the red gunstock was Michael Heraghty and it was alleged that the page from the child's copybook belonged to Mary McGranaghan who attended Cashel Glebe School, Fanad. This resulted in Michael Heraghty and the McGranaghan brothers Anthony, Thomas and Bernard being accused and placed before the July assizes. In the end no case was found against Anthony McGranaghan who was discharged while the others were placed in Lifford Jail awaiting a full trial.

Then came a strange turn in events – Michael Heraghty died of fever in Lifford Jail and the investigation by Inspector Peter Carr ran into difficulties with reports that enquiries in Fanad could make no progress because of the reaction of the local folk. Carr had gambled on the red gunstock and the child's copybook page as key clues and he had worked with meticulous precision combing the crime scene and interviewing suspects but it was deemed that not enough concrete information was available. Nonetheless it was a great example of early detective work.

However, with reward money unclaimed and with no new evidence the remaining two suspects were placed on indefinite bail. Taking the train from Strabane to Derry they arrived amid crowds of sightseers and well-wishers before boarding the Lough Swilly train to Fahan and the ferry across Lough Swilly to Rathmullan and home to Fanad.

The three assailants were never named and apart from Michael Heraghty, the other two – Neil Shiels and the red-bearded Michael McElwee were never arrested.

Yet Inspector Peter Carr would not be beaten. The ace up his sleeve was the unclaimed reward money and with this he turned to the adroit Milford solicitor William Martin.

Leaving Martin's investigations for the moment I want to turn to my BBC documentary on the *Killing of Leitrim*. Since the assailants had never been revealed publicly I would need to produce something startling, bring something extra special to the tale.

Firstly, with the information mentioned above I contacted Liam Dolan whose book on Lord Leitrim gives an excellent insight to the whole affair; secondly, I spoke to Dr.Leslie Lucas whose history *Meevagh Down the Years* has an in depth chapter on Lord Leitrim's assassination – both authors agreed to speak with me. My brother Bernard, artist and teacher, who knew Donegal well, offered to take me to the spot in Cratlagh Wood where the assassination took place.

Then, somewhat tentatively I rang H.V.Strutt (the Hon. Hedley Vickers Strutt) who had inherited Manor Vaughan from the 5th Earl of Leitrim (who had no children so the title died with him in 1952 and the estate went to the Hon. Strutt). To my surprise the Hon. Strutt said he would be delighted to be interviewed about the 3rd Earl – I was invited to Manor Vaughan.

My thoughts now focused on Dublin where the 3rd Earl was interred – surely I must view the remains, which were in the crypt of the wonderful ancient church of St. Michan's along the River Liffey's left bank not far from Phoenix Park and Dublin Zoo.

Before I departed a friend set off for Fanad to ask someone whose forebear had been directly connected with the assassination if he would agree to be interviewed – if so it would be a first and sensational with it.

In Dublin I made my way down through Temple Bar to the Liffey's right bank and over the Ha'penny Bridge then left along the quay and a few minutes stroll brought me to St Michan's Church. This gracious old edifice, which is on a site going back to 1095, is famous for Handel rehearsing the Messiah on its beautiful organ; also for the breath-taking wooden carving on the front of the organ loft. Yet probably St. Michan's is most known for the mummified bodies in its crypt – apparently the grain of the limestone dries the air and preserves the remains of many of Ireland's old families that lie here.

The verger, suitably dressed in a full length black cassock, welcomed me warmly in his soft Dublin accent and led me round to the back of the church where two solid iron covers guarded the entrance to stone steps leading down to the crypt. I have to say it was weird – the light was poor but enough to reveal the crypt as a long dark tunnel with small vaults let in to right and left along its entire length. In these vaults were stacked coffins hundreds of years old; many had split open so that bones had spilled out – the coffins were ancient looking some covered in red velvet with brass straps – in all I found it very grisly.

Did Bram Stoker get his inspiration for *Dracula* down here? That is one of the traditions of St. Michan's.

About half-way along the crypt the verger stopped and opened the door to the Leitrim vault, which was protected by a set of iron bars. Then, my heart skipped a beat or two as he spoke:

> *'In this plain oak coffin is the body of Lord Leitrim; so hated was he that before being placed here the mob tried to throw his remains into the Liffey…'*

This was no ornate coffin. It was no more than a massive plain wooden box – I had heard that Lord Leitrim was tall and strong and here was the proof – and yet here too was the fate of a wealthy man who resolute in governing his estates and paid the ultimate price.

It was impossible for me not to think what the remains were like – would the skull be smashed as was reported – how had he been laid out? My questions would never be answered because it was sealed. Nonetheless we chatted away in that bizarre setting.

I thanked the verger sincerely. Never was an interview more fitting – never more atmospheric and blood curdling. With that I made my way into the heart of Dublin – my encounter with the 3rd Earl of Leitrim in St. Michan's crypt never to be forgotten.

Next to the writers Liam Dolan and Leslie Lucas, who gave interviews that proved most valuable. Liam Dolan's excellent account gave me a detailed picture of the growing tensions in Fanad and the eventual decision to carry out the assassination including the routes taken. From Leslie Lucas I gained an insight into Lord Leitrim's unbending personality even though his intentions were genuine. Interestingly the earl was very generous in his Will to his servants although he cut most of his close family out of any entitlement.

Slowly I was getting a picture of that day in 2 April in 1878 that sent reverberations throughout the length and breadth of Ireland≈– and it became startlingly real when my brother Bernard and I visited the exact spot in Cratlagh Wood where the assassination took place. To this day it looks much the same as it did all those years ago.

Now to one of the major developments in my tale – a visit to Lord Leitrim's home at Manor Vaughan – yes, where he had set out from on that fateful day – I would encounter the Hon. H.V. Strutt.

I met him first at the estate office – tall and distinguished, we chatted easily and he was well aware of the life of Lord Leitrim and his assassination.

'Lord Leitrim was trying his best,' he declared. 'But that's not to neglect the other side of the story with the cruel treatment of the Fanad tenants.'

He spoke very well, very balanced, and in all he made an excellent contribution to my investigation. We had a stroll about the estate and later I had the opportunity to see inside Manor Vaughan – darkish interior I felt and with a gallery all the way round the entrance hall. It was from here that Lord Leitrim had set out on 2 April 1878 – but where was the clock? You see part of the story I uncovered was that the house clock had been put forward an hour so as to get Lord Leitrim on the road before his usual police escort would arrive. Perhaps it was doubtful anyway for I cannot imagine his lordship being without a personal timepiece of his own. Further information circulating was that the horse of the second carriage following behind had been deliberately lamed so to have it a distance behind Lord Leitrim's conveyance as it reached Cratlagh Wood. If so it would indicate very intricate planning and involvement stretching as far as Milford from where the vehicle had been booked.

The plot was thickening as the saying goes and suddenly the final piece of the jigsaw fell into my lap with the news from Fanad that a man whose family had been directly connected with the assassination had agreed to be interviewed under conditions of secrecy. Never before had the names of the assassins been publicly discussed in this way – oh yes, there were names passed about and suppositions made as rumours did the rounds – this was the vague way the Leitrim affair had been left down the years but that was as far as went. Now I found myself driving on a winter evening to a location in Fanad to which I was directed. One can understand my apprehension – who would I meet – what would be revealed?

It was a big house on its own – if you were to ask me now could I lead you there the answer would be no – I would not have the foggiest idea how to find it.

A stocky man, not young, invited me into a big farmhouse kitchen. The atmosphere was warm – a nice open turf fire, a ticking clock, the pleasant smell from the paraffin lamp and good solid furniture. We sat down opposite one another at a table and I switched my recorder to 'on'. Our eyes met. There was not the slightest hesitation as he spoke and suddenly it was as if I were at Cratlagh Wood all those years ago…

'Oh yes, my grandfather was there… The fatal blow? It had to be done with the butt of a gun at the wind up…that's how it finished – that's the way it was.'

It was startling – precious information and a riveting interview.

Readers studying the tale as I have related it will now be able to make judgements about the killing of Lord Leitrim. It is intriguing how the red gunstock haunts the story – *'It had to be done with the butt of a gun at the wind up…'*

Yet Heraghty, the man who owned it was not there to see it wielded. That left two others; one it was rumoured had to shave off his ginger beard because the dead Lord Leitrim was holding a tuft of it in his hand. The other was the grandfather of the man sitting opposite me.

And what of the Milford solicitor William Martin who was tasked by Inspector Peter Carr to get to the bottom of the affair quietly and unobtrusively? Who would know more than a solicitor living in the heart of the community – one who would be representing some of those under suspicion in matters of eviction and the like? With a pocketful of sovereigns Martin went about the work listening to gossip around firesides, whispers in pubs and the usual banter at markets and fairs.

His report is now tucked away in the National Archives but what he came up with is intriguing yet problematic…

'I have satisfied myself beyond doubt that the three assassins at the killing were – Michael Heraghty, Michael McElwee (Mickey Rua) and Neil Sheils… McElwee was the man who inflicted the death wound on Lord Leitrim's head with 'butt end' of Heraghty's gun… I prefer not

giving the names of the persons through whom I have been guided but what I have stated can be relied on with perfect confidence…'

No! According to all sources this was not correct. So the question remains why did such an astute man couch a report containing information that does not match what is in other meticulous accounts?

Readers may wish to wonder why this might be?

Finally to my little stroll with the Hon. H.V. Strutt at Manor Vaughan as the evening light was drawing in and the rooks were roosting in the trees…

'What do you make of it all?' I asked.

'Lord Leitrim was set on a course from which there was no escape,' said he.

'So where do you think he is now?' I continued.

'Up above perhaps,' he replied glancing Heavenwards. 'Maybe looking down… with a rueful smile at what might have been.…'

He had a nervous little laugh at the thought of it and with that we shook hands warmly and parted – he into his lonely life in Manor Vaughan and me to the long haul home.

Note: I used Vaughan Williams' *Theme of Thomas Tallis* as the music throughout my documentary – it is a very enigmatic and atmospheric piece. The programme was very well received and was mentioned in historian Jonathon Bardon's *History of BBC Northern Ireland*.

The Lady in the Moon

You must make women count as much as men…
(Emeline Pankhurst, Suffragette)

Next time you look up at the moon think how remarkable it is that one of its craters is named after a girl from this part of the world – the *Maunder Crater* – so named after Annie Scott Dill Maunder (nee Russell) formerly of Strabane County Tyrone.

Annie was an astronomer of unparalleled genius and became Annie Russell Maunder upon her marriage to astronomer Walter Maunder after the death of his first wife. Annie was extraordinary for her scientific brilliance and for the lifelong partnership with her husband that led to the discovery of unknown features of the sun and our planetary system.

Often Annie's discoveries had to take second place to her husband's because she was living under the constraints of attitudes to women in Victorian times.

Both Annie and Walter grew up within very religious families a feature that shaped the loving relationship throughout their lives and was always apparent as they travelled all over the world in pursuit of scientific exploration.

I want to take you back in time to what is known in Strabane as the Derry Road the year being 1868; here, in the new Presbyterian manse was born Annie Scott Dill Russell to parents William and Hessy.

William was the minister of the Presbyterian Church in Strabane until 1882 and Hessy was the daughter of a minister at the same church. In the end there would be six children in the family, two of them from William's previous marriage. As one might guess this was a thoroughly religious household based on strong Christian principles and engendering an ethic that education was food for the soul. All of the children were academically brilliant – Annie even in childhood displaying an unbelievable talent in mathematics.

Annie's early education would have been at the Strabane Girls' Presbyterian School, Meetinghouse Street. About the age of 14 she attended the Ladies' Collegiate School, Belfast – the school, which had a boarding department was later (in 1887) renamed Victoria College in honour of the Jubilee Year of Queen Victoria.

Annie was a dedicated pupil and gained the prize for outstanding achievement in 1886; she then obtained a three-year scholarship to Girton College, Cambridge University – this college was set up to educate women to degree level. Here in 1889 she achieved top place in the Mathematical Tripos but could not be awarded her degree because female students were prohibited from receiving these awards.

Such treatment of women was something that blighted Annie's progress over succeeding decades.

In researching the 1800s I can find no justification for why girls and women were treated in this way – not only were degrees denied them but every effort was made to prevent women inheriting their husband's estates – if there were no boys in a family the estate went to the eldest son of a brother and so on. Incidentally, in pursuit of women's rights it is worth noting that Emeline Pankhurst is reported to have visited Derry in October 1910 on a tour organised by Irish suffragettes to promote the Votes for Women campaign. (This visit is sometimes taken to be by Sylvia, Emeline's daughter).

The outcome of the lack of regard for women must have called for the greatest of patience on Annie's part for often her work had to be presented under the authorship of her husband Walter – himself an outstanding astronomer working at the Royal Observatory

Greenwich. It was here too that Annie found herself after a brief stint in teaching. She joined as a 'Lady Computer'. Such skilled assistants were paid a measly £4 per month and one of Annie's close friends at the Observatory was Northern Ireland and Girton girl Alice Everett (1865 – 1949) who had no doubt encouraged Annie to join her at Greenwich.

Annie was attached to the Solar Department of the observatory where her mathematical skills converted recorded observations into useable data. She also was introduced to a special type of telescope made for photographing the Sun. Her responsibilities were to track the movements of sunspots and to photograph the sun – something that really marked the beginning of Annie's recognition as an expert in Solar activity.

Solar Minima and Maxima are the two extremes of the Sun's activity cycles and while Walter Maunder worked on the Minima Annie concentrated on the Maxima. In July 1892 she discovered a giant black spot on the sun which resulted in a magnetic storm and by 1894 her work on the Maxima brought about tracking and identification of a high number of sunspots and the influence of these on the earth's weather. She also was appointed editor of the Astronomical Society's journal, which she continued to hold for 35 years.

In 1895 Annie married widower Walter Maunder with whom she had been working in the Royal Observatory. As a result she had to resign her post but unofficially she continued to help Walter part of their work being to further explore the influence of sunspots on the earth's weather. Annie was 27 when she married Walter who was 45. They had no children together but Walter had five children by his first marriage, the oldest 18 the youngest still an infant. Annie was no stranger to large families and soon learned to balance care for the children alongside her scientific work. Her nature was described as very lively with a wonderful imagination and a tireless zeal in seeking evidence and working out details.

Despite her lack of recognition on account of her gender the two continued to collaborate and took part in five eclipse expeditions, which included Finland, Norway, Mauritius and India – at times they had to fund trips by themselves and often made discoveries outstripping the work of nominated officials.

Speaking after the Indian trip Annie said light heartedly '… when I saw the sun's eclipse in 1898 it seemed to me as if a child had been playing the game of 'Loves me, loves me not.'

Meanwhile although she was regarded as one of the leading astronomers of her time because she was a woman her contribution continued to be underplayed. An example was her application (with two other women) to become a member of the Royal Astronomical Society, which was not granted until 1916 even though she had applied in 1895. In the intervening period she produced groundbreaking discoveries in relation to sunspot activities and their influence on the earth.

To aid her observations she designed a special telescope and lens, which was well ahead of anything else in the field at the time. Then, and most likely because of the young family around them, in 1908 Annie and Walter published a book aimed at stimulating an interest in astronomy among the wider public – *The Heavens and their Story in 1908*. Afterwards Walter graciously said, 'The book, which stands published in our joint names is almost wholly the work of my wife Annie.'

The Heavens and their Story looks at each of the planets in turn as well as the Moon and comets and concludes by looking at stars in other constellations and nebulae. It is still available to this day.

An insight into Annie's tenacity despite the restrictions on women came when Walter was sent to Mauritius – 'I determined to accompany him, and to take with me the instruments which we had used in our joint observations,' said Annie. As usual in little time her expertise was being called on.

The great partnership in marriage and scientific research between Annie and Walter lasted for 33 years. Walter died in 1928 at the age of 77 and Annie would outlive him by almost another two decades passing away aged 79 in Wandsworth, London in 1947.

Her work on sunspot observations laid the foundations for our understanding of solar activity and the Sun–Earth connection. In recognition of the contribution to astronomy by both Annie and Walter, the Maunder impact crater on the Moon is named after them. And late in the day the Royal Astronomical Society established the Annie Maunder Medal (2016) for her outstanding contribution to astronomy – much of her discoveries being still relevant in our modern world.

Annie is one of a unique band having two Blue Plaques to her name – one to her and Walter is at their former home in London and the other in her home town of Strabane.

In the year 2018 the Royal Observatory Greenwich named its new telescope after Annie.

Strange Tales to Tell

The Mystery of the Viaduct Disaster

It's coming up the valley at us…

No words can describe the beauty of the scenery – Ireland's best; but the railway journey in this part of Donegal could be terrifying.

Even today with the railway long gone the piers and pillars of the Owencarrow Viaduct present a daunting, indeed frightening prospect, as giant-like they straddle the valley on the way to Burtonport on Donegal's west coast. This wild and beautiful country through which the Owencarrow River wriggles its way saw tragedy on the night of 25 January 1925.

At the best of times engine drivers feared crossing the quarter of a mile long viaduct because of the way the wind sometimes quickened as it blew in from the ocean up the funnel shaped valley at Barnes Gap – part of what is known as the Gweebara Fault.

It was in 1903 that the Swilly Railway Company launched the Letterkenny – Burtonport Extension opening the way to journeys from Derry to the west Donegal port. As a narrow gauge railway it was ideal for going up and down the hilly Donegal countryside and a godsend to travellers when roads were so poor. Burtonport, an important fishing town on the west coast of Donegal, was in what was called a Congested District – building a railway was central to the area's development.

Without a shadow of a doubt this was one of the most

spectacular railways in Ireland. Out of Derry avoiding the coastal areas, the narrow-gauge line ran west from Letterkenny, then north by Kilmacrennan and Creeslough from where it headed west again to the magnificent Mount Errigal and the Derryveagh mountains, after which, crossing moorland and bogs, it eventually reached Gweedore and Burtonport.

The only drawback was crossing the valley on the stretch between Kilmacrennan and Cresslough. The track went down an incline on the Kilmacrennan side then crossed the viaduct over the Owencarrow River to a narrow cutting on the far side that had been blasted out of rock – here there were barely inches for the train to pass.

Some years ago I had the opportunity to talk to many of those involved on that dreadful night of 25 January 1925 – including the fireman 80 year old Johnny Hanigan, Mannix McGuinness son of the engine driver, Phil Boyle a survivor, and folk who knew the line intimately like former Letterkenny stationmaster Rory Delap. Now I want to build a picture of what really happened – the first time I have done this in print.

Picture now the flurry of activity on the platform of the Graving Dock Station on Derry's Strand Road as the 5:15pm, the so-called Bread Train, prepared for departure – fresh loaves from Stevenson's and Brewster's bakeries are piled high in two wagons behind the engine; there are three passenger carriages, goods wagons for Letterkenny and finally the guard's van – the province of Charlie Mullan who would be with the train as far as Letterkenny. On the engine footplate are driver Bob McGuinness, a man with 20 years' experience as a driver and fireman Johnny Hannigan a dozen years with the Swilly line.

'Five minutes men,' says Charlie Mullan who has come alongside the footplate. 'We've barely 20 travellin'. What do you think of the weather Bob?'

'I'm thinking we'd all be better home in bed Charlie. That wind's getting up.'

'Burtonport's four hours away. You've a wee wait for bed yet – I'll give you the go in a minute or so,' says Charlie turning back to his guard's van and with the platform clear he blows his whistle.

Imagine now we are on the footplate as Johnny fires up and Bob McGuinness slowly lets the brake off. Engine fourteen gives a shudder blasting mighty bursts of smoke and steam into the air – we are off. Some folk say these little trains stop at every hole in the hedge but with so few about on this wild evening the main stops are Letterkenny, Kilmacrennan, Cresslough and Burtonport.

Letterkenny at 6:15 sees a few passengers off, goods wagons decoupled and at 7:00pm Neilly Boyle who has replaced Charlie Mullan gets the train underway for the short distance to Kilnacrennan. The train now consists of a single wagon, three carriages and the guard's van. There are 14 passengers.

'That wind's rising, Johnny,' says Bob, 'we'll have to see how things are at Kilmacrennan.'

The journey to Kilmacrennan is more or less uneventful; John is busy keeping up the steam pressure while Bob is straining his eyes as he peers through the small porthole windows at the track ahead.

As the train moves slowly it is time to think about the folklore of the line over the years. Firstly, these night journeys into the heart of Donegal take the utmost concentration – the countryside totally dark, the only light being from oil lamps on the front of the engine. It is not unusual for foxes, badgers and the like to cross the line – I have heard also that occasionally someone is seen on the line – this reminiscent of the legend of the Urban Hitchhiker – someone who appears and mysteriously disappears. Who this is or perhaps better said what it is on the Swilly line is not known? Perhaps a harbinger of doom?

There have been rumours of sightings of a mysterious old man talking to passengers on the platform at Derry and Letterkenny during the weeks before the disaster; also there are reports of sightings of an old man walking along the Burtonport Extension and he is thought to have appeared on the night the train approached the viaduct – such sightings were believed to be that of the ghost of an individual killed during the building of the Extension.

Whatever the case it adds to the notion, whether superstition or otherwise, that crossing the viaduct was always greeted with apprehension.

Anyway, at Kilmacrennan, after listening to opinions on the state of the weather Bob McGuinness decides he will slow to 10mph at Barnes Gap, hold the engine from quickening down the incline and proceed across the viaduct as slow as he can make it.

Picture now as the train pulls on to the viaduct; the wind is getting stronger whistling and wailing through the engine wheels like a banshee, the wheels themselves go clack, clack, on the rails – it is heart-in-the mouth time.

Bob is all concentration – 'Almost there Bob…nearly into the cutting,' says Johnny, glancing back at the waggons and carriages behind them.

But then, in the distance a terrible roar. It is as if a bigger wind has come on top of what is already blowing – growling like a beast it is approaching fast.

Johnny looks at Bob and cries – 'My God, what's that! It's coming up the valley at us.'

A living nightmare is about to unfold.

The train is just within a few yards of the cutting – almost clear of the viaduct when a massive gust hits two of the carriages pitching them high in the air. One somersaults with its roof smashed to matchwood, the occupants thrown down into the rocky ravine 40 feet below. The other is left hanging precariously over the parapet, which itself is broken away by the force of the falling rubble. However, the engine, now into the cutting, holds fast.

It has happened in seconds but the aftermath is calamitous.

Cries for help are drowned by the screeching of the wind now at gale force; great sheets of rain drive in upon them.

Ashen faced Bob turns to Johnny gasping, 'My God son there's trouble the night!'

But John is in shock for out of nowhere an old man in a black cape is staring in at them screaming – 'This is terrible! This is terrible!'

With that he simply disappears – vanishes in front of their eyes.

They both glance at one another as Johnny whispers – 'In the name of God, Bob, how can it be? Sure there's no space for that man to be between the cutting and the engine. Don't like it!'

'Deal with it later. Get down to the guard's van and see if Neilly's all right. I'll check the carriages.'

Neilly's van is jammed against the parapet but Johnny manages to pull him free. 'Get to Cresslough for help – run Johnny – run!' he urges, 'I'll look for the injured.'

All of the above I obtained from my interview with Johnny Hannigan, including the sighting of the strange figure.

Now I come to what I have learned from others.

Exhausted, John sprinted the three miles to Creeslough station where he told of the accident. There was no scarcity of willing helpers; priests and doctors were quickly on the scene. As one might expect rescue efforts were hampered by the gale force winds and heavy rain, the only lighting available was provided by hurricane lamps, and keeping them alight was a problem.

It was chaos. Already three dead were recovered – Philip Boyle of Arranmore Island, Úna Mulligan and Neil Doogan, while Sarah Boyle Phil's wife suffered horrific injuries and died a short while later in Letterkenny Hospital. All were in the first coach. Phil Boyle Junior collected from Letterkenny hospital by his parents was thrown clear of the rocks and found wandering in a dazed condition. Apart from young Phil, nine other travellers were injured.

Recalling the weird figure who had screamed at Johnny and Bob – 'This is terrible!' It seems the strange hand of fate was well at work on that night.

Earlier guard Neilly Boyle chatted with Phil Boyle on the platform, along with his wife Sarah and Phil junior just out of hospital. As a result of a delay in young Phil's discharge they missed the previous train. Mrs. Boyle did not want to travel on the night train with the wind rising but was persuaded to board. This was also the case for Úna Mulligan of Falcarragh who, fearing the wind stepped off the train, changed her mind and boarded again. Also unfortunate was Neil Doogan, who lived not far from the viaduct and usually got off at Kilmacrennan when travelling from Letterkenny. Thinking the wind would be fully against him he decided to stay on the train as far as Creeslough and then walk home with the wind at his back. Neil was found badly injured and died at the scene.

Having spoken to Johnny Hannigan – such a lively and gracious man, I was then fortunate to get in touch with Phil Boyle (Young Phil) who now lived in America and was well into middle age. His parents who had collected him from hospital were both killed and he painted a distressing picture of the aftermath – he was discovered wandering in a daze under the viaduct, which was very dangerous because of the Owencarrow River and the many large deep holes filled with water. Our conversation was very emotional; even such a long time after the accident he vividly recalled the shock and heartbreak of it all – falling through the roof of the carriage – then a blank and finding himself back in hospital again – and of course inconsolable about the loss of his parents. In truth Phil Boyle – young Phil, as he was at the time, never really got over it.

My other researches brought me in contact with railway experts who had a knowledge of the line and the viaduct and I also spoke to Burtonport folk who travelled regularly on the route. Rory Delap the former Letterkenny Stationmaster gave me a thorough picture of that fateful night with many memories of the route and the people who travelled on it.

The overall impression from all I chatted with was of concern about taking the train in anything but settled weather – even then it was one of the most bone-shaking journeys one might ever imagine.

When affairs settled afterwards the Coroner's Inquest in Cresslough attributed no blame to the train personnel. The Board of Trade Engineer, Thomas Batched, was able to calculate the speed of the wind that night after extensive analysis and it was deemed that certain safety precautions were needed in future. Heavy ballasts were put on all trains using this section and a wind gauge was erected to measure wind velocity. It is said that on the night of the accident the wind was in excess of 100 m.p.h.

Despite the 1925 derailment the train service continued until the beginning of the second World War when coal shortages reduced its regularity. The last passenger train from Letterkenny to Burtonport ran in June 1941 and the line finally closed for all traffic in 1947.

Not long after the disaster Johnny Hannigan was made up to engine driver – following his father before him – Johnny's boast was that his father, suitably uniformed in white, was the driver of the train that took King Edward VII from Buncrana to Derry's Graving Dock Station in 1903.

Mannix McGuinness, Bob's son, told me his father never really got over the disaster – always wrapped up by the fire against the cold of a winter's night he would say to him -' See son – this is what the viaduct did for me.'

The Cabina Affair

One of the joys of historical researching is being on the brink of discovery of facts that have eluded one – when all appears to be lost suddenly a little jewel of information appears out of the blue and everything opens up – yet it may take time – sometimes years. This is the case for the Cabina Affair – a tale that is beginning to unfold but still needs digging about in the dusty archives.

It is a highly intriguing story.

The first inkling of a mystery came at a meeting of the Hervey Heritage Group – folk who promote the life and times of Frederick Hervey, the eccentric Earl Bishop of Derry (1730 -1803) – a larger than life character – builder of great houses, avid collector of fine art, and Continental traveller with a special love of Italy. He lived in a Rome that was eternally glorious – La Citta Eterna – yet full of wickedness – after all did not all roads lead to Rome – beautiful palaces and churches, magnificent squares, ancient ruins and teeming life? Here he could indulge himself and apart from his colourful existence his art treasures would have been worth billions in today's money.

Upon Hervey's death in Italy, Harry Bruce, a first cousin once removed, inherited his great mansion on the Downhill cliff top above the Atlantic Ocean.

In a discussion in the Hervey Group about Downhill it happened that a member revealed her great-grandfather was Joseph (Giuseppe) Cabina who as an 18-year-old boy had been taken from Lazio outside Rome by Harry Bruce (Sir Henry Hervey Bruce) and installed at Downhill.

So, why was this youth brought to Ireland?

The answer possibly lies with the Earl Bishop. When he died in 1803, Harry Bruce travelled to Italy to arrange for the settlement of his outstanding debts incurred by extensive purchases of old master paintings. While this appears to be the principal reason for Harry's trip, taking the boy back to Ireland also seems to have been part of his plans.

It was suggested that the boy was brought from Rome to improve his lifestyle and work for the Bruces, perhaps as a servant or coachman.

The 'why?' of this looms large. Downhill was not short of helpers – Harry had a family of his own and there would be no want of young men locally willing to serve the Bruces. So was Harry doing something agreed with the Earl Bishop after the boy Giuseppe was born in 1785 and now that he was 18 more suited to travel?

Harry Bruce was the Earl Bishop's loyal servant managing his affairs in Ireland and while Hervey was in Rome the pair were in continual contact by letter. Thus there was no want of dialogue between them.

Frederick Hervey was no saint especially in his later life. He left for Italy in 1791 mainly spending his last 11 years in Rome residing in Strada Felice at the Spanish Steps. Reports show him living with two women and I have found a note where he orders a crate of Chianti from his wine merchant; thus it would seem his life in Rome was rather dissolute.

So does bringing the boy to Ireland suggest an obligation to the Cabina family?

Hervey does seem to be a leading candidate for this – some opinions even express the possibility of a 'love' child – namely, Giuseppe Cabina,

The state of Italy at the time might also provide a possible clue about the boy's removal. After the French invasion in the early 1800s there were frequent disputes and uprisings concerning politics, religious tolerance, Freemasonry, and Italian unification. If the Cabinas were caught up in any of this bringing the boy to Ireland under the sponsorship of Harry Bruce would appear to be a sensible move – Bruce being able to act as sponsor for his alien status.

Yet as I delved into this intriguing story I found a twist in the tail – the plot thickens. It turns out that Giuseppe Cabina had a younger brother called Luigi (born c.1798) and unbelievably he was brought to Ireland as well – this time into Dublin; his sponsor as yet has not been identified.

The question here is did Hervey also have a connection or obligation to Luigi?

In a bid to throw light on the affair I turned to the Alien Records, which show incoming foreigners. Those for the early 1800s not being digitised were impossible to read but looking at later entries I found something astonishing. Both brothers had gone back on trips to Italy – Giuseppe to Rome and Luigi to Rome and Naples – and upon returning to Ireland both were named as couriers.

This is a mysterious development.

Couriers were used at the time because they were quicker and more private than the post; yet information on what the Cabinas were carrying is not stated. How is it that these two brothers living apart are both named as couriers – Giuseppe now a servant at Downhill and Luigi at Howth in Dublin doing farming work?

Surely one must conclude that the sponsors and /or the brothers were in contact with one another or else it is a remarkable coincidence. What they were at as couriers is yet to be determined.

Perhaps 'courier' is a badge of convenience? Yet I cannot imagine that the Bruces had any business in Italy rather than something connected with the Earl Bishop. Later Luigi travelled with and on behalf of Sir Charles Edward Kennedy – a wealthy landowner resident outside Dublin but again there is no mention of what they were up to.

To bring this together then two young brothers were brought from Italy to Ireland in the early 1800s one to Downhill and one to

Dublin. The main connection with Italy up to 1803 was Frederick Hervey known as the Earl Bishop. The boys had good conditions in Ireland – Giuseppe eventually running Downhill House for the Bruces and Luigi living at Howth and in farming.

Did the Bruces know the Kennedy family and with the latter collaborated in importing the two boys? While unlikely it cannot be ruled out – however, there may have been an earlier sponsor in Dublin as yet to be revealed. Like a good 'whodunnit' it is hard not to see Frederick Hervey's 'fingerprints' all over this tale – even though he died in 1803 he certainly could have known the boys and their father Francisco who was born c.1770.

To sum up I feel it is very unlikely that the Bruces would not have known of Luigi in Dublin and likewise those in Dublin must surely have known of Giuseppe at Downhill.

That the boys did well out of coming to Ireland there is not the slightest doubt. Giuseppe was steward and general factotum at Downhll; he was given a house and farm to rent and land of his own. Also, he was able to open a bank account and became a member of the Freemasons. Luigi did well too – owning a beautiful house on the Hill of Howth in Dublin as well as his farming activities.

Both brothers married and produced good and successful families. Also interesting is that Giuseppe became a Protestant while Luigi stayed a Catholic. Further Giuseppe is anglicised to Joseph and Luigi to Louis.

What we have then is a jigsaw puzzle with several of the pieces missing. Researchers in Rome have been unable to throw light on the Cabinas pleading great difficulty with the 1700s records. However, one must imagine that the business of sending the boys to Ireland was discussed in both Rome and Ireland and also mentioned in correspondence. To date I have seen Joseph mentioned in Bruce correspondence in relation to running the Downhill house and Louis recorded as a courier for Charles Kennedy alongside his farming.

My next move is closer scrutiny of Bruce and Hervey correspondence at PRONI (Public Records) and establishing if the

Cabinas still living in Dublin have anything on Louis.

When I stand back and survey all that is known I cannot help getting the feeling that the answer is staring me in the face though as yet I cannot see it. I hope readers will also have a go at solving this little whodunit.

Perhaps the Earl Bishop is staring down at us and wondering what our next move will be. No doubt it would bring a smile to his face and appeal to his impish sense of humour. For me it is back to the dusty archives in my bid to solve the *Cabina Affair*.

Down at the Ivy Church

Here rests his head upon the lap of earth a youth to fortune and to fame unknown… (Grey's Elegy)

A stand-off between Church and Kirk, ancient monks, a burn that pleases itself where it flows and a beautiful old-world graveyard – all part of the glorious Glendermott Valley wherein sat the Ivy Church.

The Ivy Church is long forgotten but if visitors to Old Glendermott Graveyard on Church Road, Altnagelvin, Derry, look to the left upon entering they will see quite a stretch of grass with nothing on it – this is where the Ivy Church once stood and beside it was a little schoolhouse that could cater for about 20 or so pupils – all gone now but such a story to tell.

What still exists near the graveyard is the *Raggedy Burn* – properly called the *Burngibbah* – a stream more raggedy than ever these days having silted up over the years. Raggedy (*Gibbah* from the ancient Irish) might well be taken as wayward or undisciplined – the stream flowing where it will through the Glendermott Valley that lies between Clondermott Hill and Slieve Kirk about half a dozen miles from Derry city. Mind you folk say there were times when the *Burngibbah* was a beautiful stream with lovely little pools where youngsters could learn to swim. It also produced waterpower to drive mills for scutching flax – this whole valley being a sea of blue flax flowers in summers past.

And what of the Ivy Church?

Fought over, burned and destroyed over the centuries, it saw its last days in the late 1800s

It was built around 1620 to cater for the newly arrived folk in the Plantation. The placement of the church well out in Glendermott Valley tells us a number of things. Firstly, there must have been a sizable congregation. Secondly, religion was important and a way of bringing people together – placed at the heart of the community so to speak. Thirdly, there must have been a reasonable access path through the valley to the church. Fourthly, most likely it was built from stones of a monastery sited here that some say dates to St. Columba's time though probably it was set up in the 11th century. Last and certainly not least one pictures a rather modest indeed basic building whose exterior walls became festooned with ivy – so affairs must have been reasonably quiet in the valley until the Revolution of 1641 when the church was laid to waste and had to be rebuilt when things eventually settled down.

The Lords of the Manor were the Skiptons of nearby Skipton Hall (now Beech Hill). They oversaw the worship, which was Anglican (Episcopalian) – the Ivy Church having a joint status with a similar church at nearby Enagh Lough with ministers and readers sharing duties.

Apart from its remarkable beauty Glendermott Valley has a presence – a sort of hallowed stillness about it and I put this down to the many generations that have lived here.

On the shoulder of Clondermott Hill above the graveyard is the townland of Crumkill, this an abbreviation of Colum Cille and an early indication of disciples of the saint c.1100 who built their monastery on the little rise (now the graveyard) above the *Burngibbah* stream. There were vast swathes of meadowland as far as the eye could see and no doubt they obtained permission from the local clansmen to be here and gave their blessing in return.

Archaeologists tell us that the modern field system hereabouts developed from the medieval period chopping and changing until the present times – so giving large and small enclosures and leaving us the most wonderful field patterns throughout the valley.

Long after the monks, Elizabethan incursions in the late 1500s saw the Ashe family put their roots down here at Ashbrook and then came the beginning of the making of the modern world we inhabit with the coming of the Plantation in the early 1600s. So the valley has been lived in by indigenous Irish, Elizabethan, Scots and English Plantation folk – a colourful melting pot of human beings.

Of course over the years, revolution apart, there were skirmishes but most of these were small beer compared to what was brewing at the Ivy Church.

A closer look at the incoming Planters reveals them made up of Protestants from the Anglican tradition mainly English and those from the dissenting and covenanting ideals of the Presbyterian tradition. Loosely, and perhaps rather simply put, it became framed as Church and Kirk – the Church saw the king as their mediator having the Divine right of God, while the nonconforming stock refuted this believing their Covenant was directly with God through the Bible and grace. As soldier Joseph Aiken notes in *Londerias* these differences were overcome at the Siege of Derry (1689) – *The Church and Kirk do thither jointly go in opposition to the common foe…*

However, long before that at the Ivy Church differences were not overcome.

As the year 1650 approached under Cromwell the Anglican Church was disestablished and Presbyterianism gained a foothold. The result was a fall-off in the Ivy Church congregation so that it became a Presbyterian place of worship led by a man of iron will in the shape of the aptly named Rev. John Will – a most unusual and dynamic man. This remarkable character swept all in front of him to the extent that many of the Anglican congregation joined him and he actually took over the curate's residence just opposite the Ivy Church.

John Will's influence throughout the area was prodigious – suddenly the dissenting tradition had the upper hand – worship, toil, and rest, being the order of the day for a decade while the Established Church looked on in despair.

There was strife, tension and stand-off over the Ivy Church and uneasiness reigned in Glendermott Valley. Church differences there might have been but when it came to working the land, good Christian behaviour meant that one had to help the other so a curious set of circumstances existed. However, with the Restoration in 1660 affairs swung back in favour of the Anglican folk; the Ivy Church was reclaimed and the Rev. Will was asked to vacate the residence. He refused to do so and it took a petition to the House of Lords to remove him in 1665. Yet with John Will went a lot of Anglican worshippers – so in many ways the Ivy Church suffered although it was open for worship again.

That it was back in business is marked with two of the oldest burials recorded in these parts – James and John Orneal (1671/72). Yet this calm was short-lived as the Jacobean army of James II surrounded Derry in 1689 besieging it for 105 days. The countryside was in fear and folk poured in from the country to the safety of the walled town leaving the Ivy Church unprotected and again laid waste as the Jacobean soldiers retreated southwards after the confrontation.

Battered and bruised the Ivy Church made a recovery of sorts until in 1753 it was decided to build a new church high up on the hill in the townland of Altnagelvin (Height of the Sparrows). From this date onwards the Ivy Church site was mainly used for burials; the final official interment before the move was a lady from the Skipton family though local families continued to use the graveyard. As for the school older folk in the early 1900s remember it still in use in the late 1800s.

The graveyard – with its ancient yew trees, is one of the oldest in the country and has that atmosphere one finds in the graveyards of Edinburgh like Greyfriars, Canongate and St. Cuthbert's. There are two pre-Siege graves, Siege heroes Murray and Mitchelburn, a grave to a young cricket hero, another to a teacher erected by his pupils and most remarkably the grave of Doctor Smyth who encouraged his young nephew William Beatty into medicine that saw him become Admiral Nelson's personal surgeon at the Battle of Trafalgar.

With such occupation over the centuries for me the location has a special feeling of its own. Spring, summer, autumn and winter – each bring their seasonal hues to this spot in the valley.

I imagine the joyful cry of the early monks in summer as they spot a salmon in the *Burngibbah* stream; playful cries of children back at autumn school; thick winter frost on blackthorn bush; and what can be more glorious than the blackbird's call and the heady scents of the warming sun of a fresh spring morn.

All of this down at the Ivy Church.

Malady at the Bridge

Back in 1861 when the news was announced that Derry was to get its first metal bridge over the River Foyle the city was abuzz with excitement. The building of Carlisle Bridge as it came to be called brought about the Waterside district as we know it today – also into existence came the main thoroughfares of Carlisle Road and Spencer Road. It was to introduce Derry to modern times and great prosperity and do away with the existing wooden bridge that swayed with the tides and shook with the wind,

Yet the project almost ended in disaster from the outset because of what was described as the *Mysterious Malady* – workers became afflicted with an unknown disease that left doctors scratching their heads.

Up to the building of the new bridge, folk could use the existing wooden bridge or the ferry – yet neither was completely safe so the plans for this new structure were widely welcomed. It was to be placed 200 yards up stream of the wooden bridge where the river was about a quarter of a mile wide and 30 ft. deep.

As to be expected it was a big talking point in Derry and something of a sensation when ships arrived at the quay with 16 giant metal cylinders, each 40ft. in length and 11ft in diameter. These were described as being for a new type of bridge construction and were known as caissons – from the French word for compartments. They would be erected vertically, fixed to the river bed and act as pillars to support the bridge.

Little did people know at the time that the caissons would be at the heart of the mysterious illness about to strike. It happened that in securing the caissons to the river bed each had to be pumped free of water and workers lowered to the bottom to dig out a solid foundation. To do this high pressure had to be maintained to keep out the water and the only way to do this was to seal the top of each caisson when the men were inside. Known as 'sandhogs' they would descend to the bottom on rope ladders and get to work with their shovels and picks digging deeper foundations. The only light was from candles and oil lamps, hens and rabbits were used to monitor the air quality; all round it was damp, muddy and unhealthy.

Things appeared to be going to plan when Dr. Cuthbert, who lived in the Waterside, got an urgent call to come immediately to the site works for the bridge. Once there he came upon a scene of utter chaos – men running about in panic. All work had ceased and his colleague Dr. Browne who had arrived before him was attempting to revive an unconscious man lying on the quayside.

Enquiries revealed that this man has been inside the caisson in the pressurised air when he felt ill and came quickly to the surface. He was taken to the infirmary but sadly passed away the following day leaving the doctors completely baffled.

Meanwhile, news of the accident quickly spread throughout the city, fuelled no doubt by reports from the many onlookers. Yet barely had the impact sunk in when word got out that several other workers had fallen victim to the same strange illness.

Over the succeeding days there were six serious cases – four of whom died and many other men complained of feeling unwell. This caused panic and excitement turned to fear as those tasked with building the bridge were faced with a problem they had never seen before and had not the slightest idea of how to address it.

In Derry talk of the *Mysterious Malady* swept through the city with not a little alarm.

The only clue for the doctors was that those afflicted had been working inside the pressurised caissons. Yet as the medical men deliberated, it took the civil engineer in charge of the project, John

Hughes, to offer a possible explanation. He had heard that coal miners working at considerable depths in pressurised chambers were often stooped when they came to the surface and suffered sickness and even paralysis. Similar episodes happened in France and the condition was eventually labelled Decompression Sickness. It was christened the 'Bends' as the stooping of the men resembled the popular womens' posture known as the Grecian Bend. It seems that rising too quickly into normal atmospheric pressure released nitrogen bubbles into the blood stream with devastating effect – thus the violent illnesses.

Apparently the Derry bridge operation required three times atmospheric pressure to keep the water from rising up the inside of the caissons. Thus Derry was one of the first bridge building locations to be affected by Caisson Disease thereafter officially termed Decompression Sickness. A decade later it would take several lives in the building of New York's Brooklyn Bridge.

The only light-hearted side of the Derry affair was that the hens and rabbits kept at the bottom of the caissons to gauge the quality of the air were completely unaffected.

The solution suggested by Dr. Browne was to slow the return of the workers to the surface and reduce the air pressure in the caissons; in this way the Mysterious Malady was at least kept in check and the building of the bridge got underway again.

It was officially opened in September 1863 at a cost of £65,000 – millions in today's money.

Carlisle Bridge was named after George William Frederick Howard 7th Earl of Carlisle. A favourite at court he was appointed Lord Lieutenant of Ireland – Queen Victoria describing him as – 'Good Carlisle, all brightness and smiles…' The Earl officially opened the bridge on 24 September 1863 by walking from the Derry side to the Waterside accompanied by the city fathers and a vast crowd of people.

Doctor Alexander Cuthbert was just 27 years of age when he encountered the Mysterious Malady. He was much praised for his medical skills and prepared a Paper on Decompression Sickness for the Dublin Journal of Medical Science – a contribution that was highly regarded at the time and still valuable in understanding an ailment that persists to this day.

Afterwards he was appointed Medical Officer for Derry but sadly died at the age of 42 after attending a person with Typhus – strangely, his nurse also died but the patient lived.

Nonetheless, Dr. Cuthburt's skills lived on. His grandson born in Belfast to his daughter Alice became the acclaimed surgeon Sir Ian Fraser – twice knighted and pioneer of penicillin. Also, Cuthbert Street, Waterside, is named after Dr. Cuthbert and apart from Carlisle Bridge, Carlisle Road is named after the 7th Earl of Carlisle.

Yet who could have guessed that Lord George Howard grandson of the 9th Earl of Carlisle and owner of the famous Howard Castle, would also come to Derry nearly 120 years later in 1982 to visit Radio Foyle as Chairman of the BBC Board of Governors. I was presenting the Morning Programme at the time and as mentioned elsewhere in this volume interviewed him live on air; he displayed nothing of the gruffness I had heard of – indeed was very pleasant and we had a most amusing chat afterwards.

The Secrets of St. Columb's Park House

A dandy bishop, doctors, educators, a famous artist and the mysterious *Lavender Lady* – the remarkable life of a great old Derry dwelling.

If stones could speak then what might we learn about the great houses of the past?

This was the question uppermost in the minds of the history group at St. Columb's Park House when they got access to the archives of the dwelling. All that was known was that it was once called *Chatham Lodge* and that it had passed to George Hill (later Sir George Hill) upon his marriage to Elizabeth Sophia Rae daughter of John Rae the owner at the time.

St. Columb's Park House sits overlooking the River Foyle in over 80 acres of parkland – glorious oak, beech and sycamore trees are everywhere and a beautiful little brook flows merrily through it into the river.

Visitors talk of the wonderful feeling of welcome and tranquillity at St.Columb's and as the archives were perused it became apparent why this might be – if not the stones then perhaps the archives would tell more.

They did and there was mystery too.

First thing to say is that when one stands back from the dwelling one can see that it consists of two houses joined together – the original late 1700s bow-windowed abode overlooking the River

Foyle was added to in 1832 with a long villa-like addition in the Italianate style – clean neat lines, elegant windows and extensive eave overhangs. Finished in white the house sits nobly in a clearing amongst the trees with the added touch of the ruin of an ancient little church nearby – monks worshipped here and originally the land was called *Cluainte* – the Meadows.

After being lived in from the late 1700s a caretaker and his family occupied St. Columb's in the 1930s; in the Second World War for a brief time it was home to American officers and thereafter it was a nurses' residence in the 1950s. From then onwards it lay empty until special funding enabled a complete refurbishment to bring it to the standards of a modern peace and social centre.

At the time of writing the abode is a few years short of 250 years old.

So what remains of all the life that has been lived at St. Columb's – what is behind the feeling of welcome and tranquillity? Is it *ghosts* of the past? 'Certain old houses demand to be haunted,' says the great writer Robert Louis Stevenson. Yet while St. Columb's Park House is reputed to have a 'real' ghost I never get the feeling that it *demands* to be haunted. Rather it is just part of the overall life that was lived here – the friendliest spirit you will ever encounter – the *Lavender Lady* as she is known is evident at times as is the ghost of a young boy in old fashioned clothes. Such is the mystery at St. Columb's.

It seems to me that a house moulds the people who live within it and in turn the people mould the house. In this way it develops a soul and a personality of its own.

The first task for the history group was to see how the house came about and to discover where the name *Chatham Lodge* came from?

Here we have to go back in time to the rolling meadows of Clooney (*Cluainte*) with the ruin of the tiny church and little else save the many trees and the brook – a place of supreme beauty. These lands had been given to the Irish Church at the Plantation [c.1600] so that it could have an income through leases and rents to maintain itself.

Records for 1778 mention the name Wilson and Pitt Kennedy in connection with a new dwelling, *Chatham Lodge*. The Pitt family of Derry were relatives of William Pitt , Earl of Chatham (known as Pitt the Elder) who had just died so it appears.

The Rev. John Pitt Kennedy purchased the lease and after a relatively short tenure moved to a new post at Carndonagh in County Donegal. Then came the family of John Rae about 1807. John Rea's great-great-grandfather was Francis Neville famous for his map of Derry during the Siege; John had served in the navy and was a wealthy local trader.

Thus apart from discovering how the house came to be called *Chatham* Lodge it can be seen that over a relatively short period of years families of substantial sanding were in occupation. The Pitts were active for decades on the civic scene while the Pitt-Kennedys produced highly successful off-spring in Law, Medicine and Education.

Yet it was the Reas who would shape the future of the house for decades to come.

The first John Rea died in 1810; that same year his son also called John married Louisa Blacker, daughter of a minister and she gave birth to Elizabeth Sophia who would become a central figure in the history of St. Columb's the house now being re-named St. Columb's after the ruin of the nearby monastery.

Tragically, the second John Rea's marriage was short-lived for in 1815 after giving birth to a second daughter, his wife Louisa passed away in Dublin at the age of just 22 years. A white marble memorial erected by John in St. Columb's Cathedral Londonderry laments her passing after *'a long and most afflicting illness'* and with this comes the first of the mysteries of the house.

Louisa had been a young teenage bride and by the wording of the memorial it would seem health wise that she had a difficult time. A common illness was TB known as the *Decline* though this is nowhere mentioned; other suggestions are that it might have been sickness during her pre-birth lying-in.

Whatever the case the various conjectures have led to the suggestion that Louisa although dying in Dublin may be the *Lavender Lady* the ghostly presence often sighted in the house and which endows it with such mystery.

Sadly, Louisa's second daughter also had a short life dying at the age of 35 in 1850.

Apart from the Reas another dimension came to the house in 1809 with the marriage of John Rae's sister Jane to the Rev. Thomas Bewley Monsell. Jane had four children; the first of these William was born at *Chatham Lodge* in 1811, followed by John, Diana and Charles.

John Monsell entered the Church, becoming Rector of St. Augustine's on the city walls and made his name as one of the leading hymn writers of his day – including *'Fight the Good Fight...'* He was a favourite of Queen Victoria and she appointed him as her chaplain at Windsor in 1875.

Meanwhile, the Rev. John's sister Diana became a renowned botanical artist the main theme of her watercolour paintings being bluebells, primroses, violets and lavender – the love of the latter making her another contender for the spectral *Lavender Lady*. Sadly, like many others who came into the world in St. Columb's she had a short life dying at the age of 38 and leaving behind a little child of six years of age.

Another early death was William the first born Monsell boy who only lived into his teens. However, the youngest, Charles, he too of poor health, went on to study medicine and against the O'Brien family's wishes eventually married Harriet O'Brien the daughter of Sir Edward O' Brien a direct descendent of Brian Boru. The marriage was both happy and tragic; Charles opted to join the ministry but died in Italy where he had gone for his health. Grief-stricken Harriet Monsell abandoned the comforts of life and founded a community of nuns dedicated to helping women who had fallen into difficult times; it gave rise to orphanages, schools and hospitals and was one of the first Anglican religious orders of its kind. Harriet died on Easter Sunday 1883 and was later listed among the Anglican Saints.

Finally, to the family with whom St. Columb's Park House became principally identified in Derry – the Hills, mainly of Brook Hall. George Hill married Elizabeth Sophia Rea (John Rea's daughter) in 1831 and as part of the transaction the dwelling and the lands became his. In 1832 he commenced the Italianate extension that is a sizable part of the present abode .

Their marriage produced six surviving children and in 1839 George Hill became Sir George upon the death of his uncle. Then with famine looming and severe conditions throughout Ireland he moved his entire family to St Helier, Jersey, where there were Hill relations. However, tragedy struck yet again. Sir George had a stroke and died in December 1845 aged 41. More was to follow with the deaths of two-year-old Francis and 13-year-old George – John, next in line, inherited St. Columb's but he too had a short life dying in his 30s.

Of the remaining family Rowley Hill born in the house in 1836 became the most outstanding being appointed Bishop of the Isle of Man in 1877. Fastidious in everything from boyhood Rowley's stylish dress as a bishop earned him the title of the *Dandy Bishop*. Ever popular he is named in a Gilbert & Sullivan operetta and passed away at the relatively young age of 51.

Throughout all the happenings at St. Columb's Park House the heroine must surely be Lady Elizabeth Sophia – maintaiining the house; seeing her children through their infancy; losing her husband at the age of 41 and her off-spring as well; and not to mention running the St. Columb's and Brook Hill estates both of which came under her remit with the death of her husband. Eventually and no doubt well worn out she retired to Brighton and died at the great old age of 91.

Incidentally, in 1842 just before Sir George left for Jersey sweeping down the long drive to St. Columb's came a visitor who was destined to become internationally renowned for his writing – William Makepeace Thackeray. The author, who was on a tour of Ireland for his *Irish Sketchbook* tells us that – '*We trotted off for Londonderry leaving at the pretty lodge of St. Columb's a letter, which was the cause of much delightful hospitality…*'

This gives rise to another of the mysteries of St. Columb's. A letter? Why was Thackeray so vague – and what was in this letter that brought him such warmth and entertainment? It is only when we retrace his earlier steps that we find he has called upon his cousin Elias Thackeray at Dundalk – he does not declare it but Elias was married to Rebecca Hill, Sir George Hill's aunt. The letter most likely about family matters of interest to Rebecca and Sir George no doubt also contained an introduction for the writer that brought '…*much delightful hospitality…*'

Yet he divulges nothing to us.

To me it hints of a very unpleasant side of Thackeray which is apparent in various ways throughout his *Irish Sketchbook* – a sort of arrogance indeed distain for the Irish even though he married an Irish girl Isabella Shawe. Thankfully and who knows maybe because of the hospitality at St. Columb's he has nothing but good to say about his experiences in Derry and its surrounds. By the way, his most famous book *Vanity Fair* was written some six years later.

Meanwhile and no doubt with sadness after the tribulations of Jersey Lady Hill took her leave of St. Columb's forever taking up permanent residence in Brighton. This makes way for the Bond's again who returned to farm the land and do so very successfully. Yet the days of the great dynasties – the Pitt Kennedys, the Reas and the Hills were over. Short term occupations came with business man and brewer John Meehan then came Dr. Barnewall White a local physician followed by the Cookes a shipping family and finally Michael Feeney a solicitor who left the house with the onset of the 1930s.

Thereafter John and Mary Nichol along with their family moved into St. Columb's as caretakers. Their son Robert writing afterwards paints a picture of what the dwelling was like:

Though neglected, there still remained an aura of the house's former opulence, from the library with its floor to ceiling shelves on all four walls, the pleasant aroma of old books still lingering in the air; the ballroom with its polished wooden floor, large shuttered windows, impressive fireplace and highly decorated ceiling. In alcoves at the bottom of the grand staircase languished two Greek goddesses. A passageway in the hall led to the kitchen and servants' quarters with small rooms on either side, bathrooms and a scullery. Large meat hooks hung from the kitchen ceiling and over an enormous fireplace were suspended pots and pans with two ovens positioned on either side of the fire. In the centre of the room stood a large well-scrubbed wooden table and along one wall was a dresser still fully bedecked with the finest crockery. With no electricity in the house, all activity was carried out under the comforting glow of oil lamps, adding their own inimitable smell to the rooms. Upstairs, there were six bedrooms, two dressing rooms and a bathroom, the family occupying the three bedrooms to the front which afforded the best view of the tree lined avenue to the house.

One of the upstairs bedrooms was chillingly cold even on the warmest day and was religiously avoided by all the family, rumours abounding that it was haunted by a young lady who had died tragically in the room, the legendary Lavender Lady.

Talked about in the most intriguing but friendly way the *Lavender Lady* still persists to this day.

In World War II St. Columb's was used by American officers before becoming a nurses' residence in the 1950s, Finally came a reincarnation for the house in the 1980s when it was completely refurbished leaving the modern and highly social centre it is today.

What better then to end a trip to St. Columb's Park House with some lines by W. B. Yeats:

> *I came upon a great house in the middle of the night,*
> *Its open lighted doorway and its windows all alight,*
> *And all my friends were there and made me welcome too…*

So Many Horrid Ghosts

The Case of the Singing Ghost

Go and catch a falling star, and teach me to hear ghosts singing…
(John Donne)

It was the most delightful voice you might ever hear its colour and depth just magical. Yet it only lasted seconds and vanished.

All of us heard it. Was it a ghost?

One of the things I've discovered in investing spooky phenomena for radio is that ghosts do not appear to order rather they come up out of the blue; suddenly they are there. Certainly this was the case for the *Singing Ghost* – unexpected, indeed, without any warning whatsoever it happened.

It came about on my early days on radio – it was coming up to Halloween and months before Radio Foyle came into being the late Roy Hamilton, a most excellent broadcaster, and I, decided to do a piece on ghosts for *What's West* the weekly BBC programme from Derry.

We aimed to travel to Lurgan to interview Sheila St. Clair an expert on all things paranormal. And so we set out. It was a long evening's journey yet Sheila made us most welcome and soon we were we chatting before a lovely fire. I must say I found her a remarkable lady agreeable in every way.

Sheila and her husband Les had recently been called in to investigate happenings in one of Belfast's old theatres where the staff had walked out having been frightened by sightings of a ghost. Theatres are renowned for tales of hauntings and Les was listening to recordings they had made during the night after the walk-out.

Sheila, apart from being a teacher, was an authority on folklore, alongside which she had researched many haunted places. Anyway, we carried out our interview, which I found intriguing but scary and not helped I might add by the presence of Sheila's beautiful Siamese cat, which jumped up on the sofa beside me as she was speaking and seemed – at least I imagined so, to look at me very curiously.

Then, even though it was getting late Sheila insisted we have tea before departing and rose to go down the passageway to the kitchen. I followed to continue our chat while Roy went into the hall to telephone his wife Marion to say he would be late home.

As he lifted the phone it happened – yes, right out of the blue there was this most delightful singing – quite distinct, melodious like an opera singer rendering a scale from low to high – an attractive, mysterious sound that lasted for a few seconds but somehow seemed to possess the very air about us so seductive an *Arpeggio* it was.

Roy almost dropped the phone; Sheila came running down the passageway and bumped into to me while Les appeared at the living room doorway – the 4 of us were stunned – absolutely speechless. We looked at one another wide-eyed and I stammered – 'What on earth was that…?'

Sheila said 'There's a reason…' To which husband Les replied – 'You mean we brought something home with us?'

'No! You know we agreed never to say such things!' responded Sheila sharply. And I can tell you if Roy and I were startled suddenly we were well and truly shaken.

We all agreed we had heard the singing and with Sheila adding that the incident should be reported to the Society for Psychical Research we took our leave – the occurrence very much unresolved.

Our journey home was very much in silence.

Days later we were wondering if Sheila might have played a trick on us it being Halloween. Yet when I telephoned her she was adamant something entirely unusual had occurred. 'Since Roy's wife Marion sang in a choir I thought there might have been some sort of connection there, 'she said.

I was not convinced. Some of Belfast's old theatres had been music halls and my thinking turned to Les's words – 'You mean we brought something home with us?'

The incident became a talking point and about a year later we decided to put the question to Sheila 'live' on air – 'Did she play a prank on us?'

'Absolutely not!' she declared and as before added that it was a happening for the archives of the Society for Psychical Research.

Over the years we have often chatted about what we eventually described as the *Singing Ghost*. Then recently I was listening to a music voice coach discussing the singing of scales. She played recordings old and new and suddenly in one of the very early music hall renderings I was transported back to that strange evening with Sheila for there was the sound of the voice – or as near as I can remember the voice that I had heard on that evening long ago.

I was dumbstruck for in a way the voice had lived on in my memory.

As to why the ghostly singing had happened all those years before I cannot tell.

What I can say is that all of us did hear it and it has come to be known as *The Case of the Singing Ghost*.

Things That Go Bump in the Night

*There are more things in heaven and earth, Horatio,
than are dreamt of in your philosophy…*
(Shakespeare – Hamlet)

Is it that noise in the corner you cannot account for when you are alone at night or perhaps the tread of footsteps on the empty stairs or furniture being moved on the floor above when you know no one is there?

Things that go bump can be frightening.

I am going to tell you about one such episode in the hope that you may be able to think what might be at the bottom of it.

It comes from the Derry author Kathleen Coyle writing in her book *Magical Realm*. Kathleen's relations on her mother's side grew up in a house in a thoroughfare that would eventually become the city's William Street. Built in the late 1700s by Thomas McNulty for his sweetheart they would marry and have a large family of girls and boys 11 in all.

It was the happiest of marriages – Thomas had eloped with his beloved and when the 11 children were gathered round them he took great pride in simply calling her mother. Thomas was well respected in Derry being one of the builders of the new Long Tower Church(1783) and on friendly terms with the Catholic bishop Dr. McDevitt and the Protestant bishop Frederick Hervey Earl of Bristol.

The McNulty boys were doted on by the girls and imagine the loss when the oldest John decided to join the Spanish army. Then absolute heartbreak when the youngest and his mother's favourite opted to go as a student cum assistant to a private school in England with the hope that he could become a teacher.

So, the young McNulty left home to further his ambition.

One can picture the sadness that hit the family. He was their pride and joy, was bright intellectually and could never do enough for his mother and the girls. His father had converted the attic into a study and bedroom for him; here he could have all his bits and pieces and keep his favourite possessions undisturbed. From his attic window with his precious spyglass he could view the sailing ships and frantic comings and goings on Derry Quay. This prized object he would keep tucked away safely in his bedside drawer.

When he left for England the room was locked; in a way it became frozen in time – a sanctuary dedicated to this well-loved young man and awaiting his return. In the meantime letters aplenty came back describing his new life, which was often exciting but with complaints that the school where he was assisting could do better for its pupils and staff.

His letters were kept in a little pile by the mantelpiece clock in the living room and from time to time the girls would spend an evening reading them. Then one winter's night after the family had gone to bed in the small hours there came a bump from the top of the house. The mother was the first to waken and only when it got louder did her husband Thomas stir.

'What on earth is that?' he gasped.

By this time mother had opened the door to the landing where she found the girls gathered in a huddle.

'What can it be, Mama?' they asked.

Thomas McNulty frowned. Having built the house he knew every square inch of it – 'It's nothing,' he said as the noise stopped. Minutes later it started again much louder.

'Goodness, Papa! ' cried the family in unison.

'I'll go up and check – all of you better stay here, 'whispered Thomas.

'No, Papa! We'll all go" came the response.

So all of them trooped cautiously behind their father making for the upper storey – the noise still loud and their only light a lantern.

Imagine the panic as they crept up that dark shadowy staircase.

When they got to the bedroom it clearly sounded as if furniture was being moved around inside and noisily too – there was no mistaking it.

Thomas looked over at his wife who crossed herself and nodded for him to continue. The key was in the lock and turning it tentatively he pushed the door open.

Suddenly there was a gush of air that rattled the windows of the house and the noise stopped abruptly.

There was silence – hearts were thumping, nerves jangling.

Yet remarkably nothing had been disturbed – the furniture was in its usual place. That is except for something…yes, something placed upon his pillow that I shall come to shortly.

Eventually they got back to bed but after breakfast mother announced with a sigh that she thought the commotion during the night was a warning – their precious boy was dead.

One can picture the effect on the family – all had heard the ghastly noise but to think the boy they loved so much was dead. Surely no…?

These were times when it could take weeks to get news but when the parish priest arrived at their door just days later he bore the astonishing word that the boy had indeed died – of pneumonia it was said not helped by the poor conditions around him at his school.

The death left a mark upon the McNulty family never to be forgotten.

And now to return to what I mentioned earlier. Something for you to consider in this strange and eerie affair. For resting on the pillow was his pride and joy, the companion of his life – his spyglass.

How did it come to be lying there on that dreadful night when it was usually kept locked away in his drawer – with key that only he possessed?

Quite simply it never could be explained – a mystery the family could never fathom and that started with a bump in the night.

Such is the story aired in Kathleen Coyle's *Magical Realm*.

Note; *The school where young McNulty attended was visited by Charles Dickens and appeared as the despicable Dotheboys Hall in his novel Nicholas Nickleby.*

Country Ghosts

Now I know what a ghost is. Unfinished business, that's what…
(Salman Rushdie)

In that stretch of land where the River Faughan flows from the Sperrin Mountains past the delightful old-world villages of Park and Claudy one finds beautiful countryside of woods, streams and rolling hills and a local tradition that talks of two ghost stories. It well befits spooky tales with gathering mist on a winter's eve, soft mauve and russet twilights and rooks roosting under frosty skies.

It seems to me that time has stood still here for it has changed very little since the 1800s when our two stories find the light of day at Learmount Castle and Cumber House.

Firstly, to Learmount between Park and Claudy. This dwelling that belonged to the Beresford family is mock Tudor with a touch of Gothic in style and commands a magnificent view over a vast forest through which winds the River Faughan. The location is very atmospheric, has a strange feel to it. Learmount Castle, so called, would easily make a chilling movie set with its tall chimneys and eerie windows from which folk of the past gazed out. Indeed it was well-lived in for over a couple of centuries and one can easily sense the life that was played out here during that time.

And what of ghosts? Hauntings apart, folk have talked about something frightening, an evil presence that lingers in the local countryside hereabouts – this we shall come to.

Yet Learmount appears to be a place of calm and solitude. It came to the Beresfords through the marriage of the Hon. John Beresford and the heiress Barbara Montgomery and stayed within the family until the estate was sold to the Forestry Service after World War II. It had been used as a temporary base for Ashfield Girls' School Belfast during the war and then became a youth hostel and centre for orienteering until the 1980s. I well remember taking school trips to Learmount and a notice just inside the door that read – *Noises that have been heard in the castle have been put down to settling within the structure…* It calmed the nerves for some – but not for all as we shall see.

Let us now go to Cumber House that sits a few miles back along the road from Learmount near Claudy. This is a fine-looking Regency style house built in 1830 or slightly before by Major John Hamilton Browne (b.1763 d. 1848); his marriage brought about the Browne-Lecky family – the Leckys being very prominent in Derry. There is an attractive park surrounding the house and an old church and cemetery nearby where the Brownes are buried. The family finally faded from the scene in the 1930s. After this it was used as a services billet during World War II and came under the management of John Mitchell's GAC (Gaelic Football Club) in the 1970s.

Ghost hunters have been to the house and spookily enough a tree close by may be related to the ghost story.

Thus with Learnount and Cumber House we have two large country dwellings associated with ghostly tales. It strikes me as interesting that they are just a few miles apart and that the timing of the hauntings is as near as can be judged somewhere around the mid-1800s or slightly after. Also, a priest and exorcism is involved in both and the spirits may be demonic.

In thinking about the tales we have to be aware that they may be coloured in the telling over the generations. Unfortunately, both are lacking in solid facts giving cynical folk good grounds for disbelief. So I relate them for people to make their own minds up as to the veracity of the hauntings.

The most substantial account that I have come across with regard to Learmount relates to a young member of the original family who lived in the dwelling in the 1700s before the Beresfords. At this time badly behaved young men were often referred to as *Squireens* – really an Irish connotation for youths engaged in outrageous conduct – gambling, drinking and the like.

This particular youth having already far exceeded the limits of good behaviour decided one day to attempt the impossible – to ride his horse up the stairs and jump from the front window unto the grass below. It must be said that Learmount at the time was much smaller – the height of the jump some 16 feet or so. Nonetheless it was a moment of madness. Incredibly he negotiated the stairs on to the landing that led to the window but then his mount thought the better of it and would go no further. The calamitous result was that the young rider was propelled through the window to the ground below where he was gravely injured and died days later. Sometime after this a malevolent presence began haunting the house – a troublesome noisy spirit it was said – and one can imagine such a manifestation in the dark stairways and shadowy corridors of Learmount.

Yet it was not until new generations and a refurbishment of the castle that a picture emerged of what the frightening spirit might be for it seems it had become much more disturbing in the 1800s.

It is said that one evening the young men in Learmount were partying when one of them suggested they might have some fun at the expense of the local priest telling him that a malevolent presence was terrifying the household. Accordingly the priest prayed for the exorcism of the spirit as the merrymakers looked on when suddenly a blast of wind rocked the dwelling from top to bottom and in the fireplace there appeared a hideous black dog – its coat leathery and slimy, its eyes blazing, its fangs bared – an evil beast that went on the rampage scattering the merrymakers and causing havoc before darting off into the night.

The priest withdrew in shock his hair turning white overnight and the incident is often recalled in these parts. A tradition in the neighbourhood and far beyond is that from that time the *Black Dog* appears. However, this menacing creature may not be witnessed in Learmount anymore for the castle is sealed up and as to the wider district there have been no further reports.

Moving on to Cumber House the tale involves one of the Browne sons and a demand that the local priest resurrect the spirit of his dead father after accusations had been made about his bad behaviour during his lifetime. Threatened at gun point in Cumber House the frightened priest drew a circle on the floor and during his prayers the apparition of the deceased man appeared in the circle surrounded by flames. The priest fled in panic and the spirit now let loose frightened folk out of their wits. Eventually, another priest was called and he exorcised the sprit by confining it to a tree, which still stands near Cumber House.

Personally, I have never heard of exorcism involving a tree. However, confining a spirit within a room or closed space is very much part of the Irish tradition of hauntings.

Folk still believe Cumber House is haunted giving rise to the question was the spirit ever banished at all? Ghost hunting groups maintain the place is still haunted but I have not come across any decisive proof that this may be so.

What is interesting about the two stories is the old-world country settings, dark intriguing big country houses, bad behaviour, the priest called – who wouldn't be waiting for something dreadful to happen?

Yet those who do not believe in ghosts will say this was the past – old-fashioned times, yarns around the fireside and superstition. Perhaps – but if folk believe in UFOs and aliens surely in tribute to the great land that we inhabit we must admit that not seeing something does not mean it does not exist.

A Haunting in Fanad

'Haunting…? All argument is against it…but all belief is for it…
(Dr. Johnson)

Fanad, lies between Lough Swilly and Mulroy Bay in County Donegal and is one of Ireland's treasured beauty spots. The restless Atlantic Ocean rules this wild and rugged place but something strange happened here in 1778 – suddenly out of nowhere a malevolent force took hold over the land.

It happened in the little townland of Drumfad and has come to be known as the *Fanad Haunting*.

If the ocean was restless around Fanad in those times so was the population too – Catholics, Church of Ireland and Presbyterian were frequently at loggerheads and plots were simmering among the United Irishmen; affairs political and religious were distinctly uneasy.

It is into the middle of this melting pot that the sinister tale of a haunting begins to unfold. Now there are many versions and distortions in relation to what was happening so I have had to tread carefully to get at the crux of the matter.

Come with me now back to those heady times – the roar of the ocean, the wail of the wind and voices raised among warring parties. One day a farmer in Drumfad rebuked the local parish priest for trespassing on his land and the pair parted with threats and angry words.

That evening something frightening happened in the farmer's household – furniture started moving of its own accord, cups and plates flew off the dresser smashing on the floor and chairs and pictures were tossed into the air. The disturbance continued off and on over the following days driving folk in the house to distraction. It seemed as if whatever was causing the disturbance had a mischievous side to it – it would play pranks, tug at folk, pull hair and make a general nuisance of itself and all the while an uneasy heaviness lay over everything.

Picture yourself in that terrifying atmosphere – what is more alarming than something that threatens yet one cannot understand why it is happening or what it will do next?

It was not long before news of the commotion spread across Fanad and further afield; soon it was reported in newspapers throughout the country and crowds came flocking to witness the rare goings on at Drumfad.

The farmer became further distressed when the disturbances spread to outside the house. Implements were hurled through the air, hay stacks were knocked over and animals were chased around fields. Indeed, the malaise was beginning to spread far and wide.

'The place is possessed,' was the word doing the rounds; and with all of this happening in a land rich in fairy tales it was not long before folk were asking what could be the cause of such weird goings-on?

I suppose in general terms it was classified as a *haunting*, that said, it has all the characteristics of poltergeist activity. Nearly every country has reports of poltergeists – *noisy spirits* – and it is amazing how similar such episodes are – objects thrown, dishes smashed, noises and often interaction with humans either threatened or subject to mischievous behaviour.

Some researchers maintain it is fraudulent while others say it is paranormal. Of course the first question that comes to mind is why should objects be thrown or upset in this way?

One assumes it is to disrupt or engender fear. Sceptics might argue the reason is to bring about something – perhaps getting folk to vacate a dwelling or maybe just to play a practical joke.

In the case of the Fanad episode eventually the farmer approached three churchmen comprising a priest, a Presbyterian and a Church of Ireland minister in the hope that they could cleanse the farm of the troublesome entity. This did not work – reports talk of the three being vilified by the entity and having to hurry away from the scene in fear and trembling. Attempts were also made to implicate a young servant girl but this came to nothing since the disturbances also occurred when she was not in the house.

Finally, the story goes that the farmer, remembering the incidents began after his argument with the local parish priest, begged him to come and exorcise the mischievous being. This the parish priest agreed to do no doubt after gaining concessions about travelling over the farmer's fields – the cause of the dispute in the first place.

It seems that the exorcism brought all forms of fire and brimstone down on the premises – the evil presence refusing to move. Yet in the end after a mammoth effort it was forced out through the door and disappeared in an adjacent field leaving a scorched hole in the earth. It is said that the spot where it disappeared can still be identified to this day.

Readers, especially those whose credulity has been tested, will not be surprised to hear that there is a twist in the tale of the Fanad haunting. It seems that long after the trouble had settled people noticed a brilliant while cockerel strutting proudly about the farm yard. It had not been seen before the exorcism and it was not long before it was being linked with it.

Apart from the parish priest it seems two men arrived claiming that they could banish the spirit. As part of their ritual it was believed they used a white cockerel the bird being regarded as sacred as far back as the ancient Greeks. The two men used the cockerel to battle against the entity, which, so the story goes, fled from the house after being confronted with the dynamic bird.

Such fanciful tales are typical of the folklore that has grown up around the Fanad haunting. One account even talks of using the paraphernalia of Free Masonry to free the house of the troublesome spirit.

So where does it leave such a haunting? The story finds the light of day in a time of religious and political upheaval – did the farmer conjure up the happenings in a way of getting back at the parish priest or did the row between them unleash or open a door to something paranormal? The tale no doubt was added to around firesides – the white cockerel giving a touch of the mystique.

Sceptics will call it superstition played out in the heart of the country in time of upheaval and dark winter nights. On the other hand it does have all the ingredients of a poltergeist at work – inexplicable happenings out of the blue, frightening occurrences and then a dropping off and finally an end to the disturbances. In the case of Fanad it lasted for two years and then stopped.

The house at Drumfad is still there and some folk will tell you that if you wait long enough the white cockerel will appear too.

The Ghost of the White Horse Inn

All houses wherein men have lived and died are haunted houses...
(Longfellow)

I have been pondering lately if ghosts go out of fashion. Maybe they take a break – lie low for a while. Certainly this seems to be the case for the ghost of the White Horse Inn. Back in the 1960s it was a regular talking point yet these days there is little mention of it.

The White Horse Inn sits on the main road at Campsie about five miles from Derry. It has a beautiful old-world feel about it. As an inn it is over 200 years at this spot having been built by Patrick Cole in 1818. Known as *Coles of Campsie* it was designed to cater for horse drawn carriages from Newtown Limavady into Derry on a new loop of road that bypassed Eglinton – the original highway through the village being unsatisfactory for the developing traffic.

Post houses, as the inn was, not only afforded changes of horses if required but also dealt with mail as well.

The Coles sold the inn in 1938. By this time it was very busy with the increase of transport to the local airports of Maydown and Eglinton constructed for the World War II effort.

Reports of a ghost go right back to the 1800s. A feature is that this is not a *haunting* of the White Horse Inn (now a modern hotel) but a phantom carriage with four white horses that draws up outside the inn.

We have to go back to the 1960s for the last major mention of the ghost. Celebrated Coleraine journalist the late 'Speedy' Moore travelled to meet a team of men who met every seven years at the inn to wait on the ghost's arrival. There was a photograph of these men in the entrance hall of the inn up until recent times; they were quite convinced that there was something to the story.

Speedy's article gives a description of the spooky happenings. Firstly, comes the sound of a carriage drawing up, horses and wheels grinding to a stop on the gravel outside the inn. There are four brilliant white horses champing at the bit and the driver, a stout man, alights and hurries up the path towards the inn door. Then suddenly he vanishes and as he does so the coach and horses disappear into thin air leaving everything in darkness.

This by tradition is what the watchers wait to see every seven years. It certainly stems from when the Coles owned the inn – that is, in the days when it was a traditional posthouse. Imagine then you are watching from the door when the coach driver comes up the path towards you. Descriptions of the carriage behind him talk of it appearing to be glowing and there is only a hint of folk inside. Then, just as you are about to step aside the driver coming towards you vanishes – absolutely disappears into this air while the carriage and horses slowly dissolve into nothing.

Apparently in ghostly folklore, apparitions of phantom carriages are fairly common and in most cases they relate to a calamity or serious happening. Since carriages were the mode of transport in the Cole's time it could well be that there had indeed been a mishap. However, as yet I have found no reports of a past disaster along the route though this in no way implies that there might not have been.

That the tale persists over such a long time one has to think that something unusual did occur. All sorts of possibilities present themselves. Was the driver rushing to get help, or report something or had there been a highway robbery or some other terrible happening? The other abiding question and one that sends a shiver down the spine is who was in the coach – was it some poor departed souls; where had they come from and to where were they going? And does this spectral appearance go on forever with those poor souls trapped there?

Such are the deliberations over the ghost of the White Horse Inn and I wonder what William Makepeace Thackeray made of the tale when he called at the White Horse Inn in October 1842 – tradition says he stopped here for some hot punch on his way into Derry. There were dark nooks and crannies in the old dwelling that I am sure had him thinking. Thackeray liked a good spooky tale and ghosts do figure in some of his work.

Mind you some of the caustic remarks for which he was famed would surely have sent the poor souls scurrying back to the world of spirit for safety.

Twist in the Tale

Silver Flash

My favourite river wriggles its way through a countryside of forests, cornfields and meadows occasionally taking a notion to hurry along with fast flowing streams before slowing down into stretches of mirror calm water and deep pools.

It is the River Faughan, clear and clean along its length, and well-named the *Sheltered Place*.

It was all of this for me until one unforgettable summer afternoon. I was 11 years old; school holidays had just begun and I had wandered out from town in the hope of meeting up with friends at our favourite swimming hole where the river curved and the trees sloped out giddily over the water. Here salmon like to lie and if you are lucky you will catch the dive of an orange and blue kingfisher that comes and goes in the blink of an eye before stillness rules. At times too you might even spot a fox or a badger. Above all there is a sense of wildness, excitement and freedom.

On this day the place was empty so I sat down on a fallen tree trunk to watch the river for there was talk of a big fish about; the water was as smooth as glass and there was always a chance that the silence would be broken with a great splash.

With talk of a big fish folk would be wondering who would get it first – the anglers or the poachers?

I was in a sort of reverie when there came the sound of breaking branches and to my dismay I spotted sinister movement further up the bank – black outlines at first and then horror as I realised that it was *Them* – the three brothers who roamed the bank night and day and detested young folk who came to swim in the river.

Dressed in blue jerseys, ill-fitting trousers and thick brown boots they were constantly on patrol, moving up and down the bank like an express train – foraging, prodding and scratching for anything they could find and above all infamous for poaching salmon. Each time they would pass us boys at the swimming hole it would be a look that spelt – 'Clear off. We don't want you here! This is our territory!'

We stood our ground but it was an uneasy situation for the swimming hole was one of their haunts for poaching when they could escape the watchful eyes of the bailiffs.

Imagine then my panic – suddenly here they were – the older in his 20s, menacing and scrawny looking, the next aged about 18 with an almost expressionless face and the younger a pleasant looking boy of about 16 – so different that I almost felt like saying to him – 'What on earth are you doing with them?' Yes, *Them* – that is indeed how we named the three who we were told lived further down the bank near the scutch mill.

'What are ye doing here?' growled the older one. 'No place o' yer own?'

I shrugged my shoulders and made to go.

'You just sit where ye are. Have ye seen anybody about?'

I shook my head.

'Ye'll be in that river if there's so much as a cheep out'o ye,' said he before snapping at the others. 'What are yees waiting for!'

What happened next I am sure was well rehearsed.

The middle one lay on his stomach with his head out over the water and shading his eyes looked down into the depths. I knew straightaway that he was looking for the big salmon who might have come in to rest under the shelter of the bank – I might add that spotting a fish like this is not easy for its back is the same colour as the river bed.

Meanwhile the younger boy had hauled himself up onto the branch of a tree and suddenly I knew what was happening – poaching! He was the look-out.

The middle one lay motionless, his feet held by the older lest he tip into the water. Then, after several minutes he nodded his head and the older placed a short length of wire with a noose-like loop on the end of it into his hand.

Slowly, ever so slowly, the wire was lowered into the water not a sound made.

My heart was thumping as the boy in the tree signalled it was all clear to go ahead. Suddenly it was as if the water exploded. Up into the air came a salmon, the noose trapping it by the tail.

This magnificent creature seemed to hold still, timeless for a moment, its body curved – a *silver flash* caught in the rays of the sun, truly a work of splendour.

Then, in seconds, it was whipped helpless on to the bank. There were whoops of delight from the brothers as the poor being was reduced from majesty as the king of the river to such a miserable state flipping and flopping about.

'A beezer boys – a beezer!' Cried the scrawny one and taking a branch struck it on the head, a blow that stopped it moving. 'A ten-pounder – the one we were lookin' for – must be two feet in it.'

As you might guess I was petrified upon seeing such a beautiful thing rendered senseless.

Yet the drama was by no means over.

'Bailiffs! Bailiffs!' Comes the sudden cry from the boy in the tree.

'Grab it and run,' urged the middle boy.

'No! We'll be seen,' snapped the older.

'Then throw it back' responded the others. 'We're for it if they catch us!'

Yet the older one is eyeing me. 'Get yer jacket off!' he demands.

'But…' I stammer.

'Hurry – or yer goin' in that river!'

He snatches the jacket from me wraps it round the salmon and putting it on the tree trunk orders me to sit on it.'

'We'll be back – an' ye'd better say nothing!'

With that they scuttled away.

Just as the bailiffs arrived my blood froze for there was movement underneath me and I swallowed hard for the salmon had come to life and was wriggling so much I felt I must scream and leap into the air. But then with one last twist it stopped, the bailiffs unaware that the pride of the river was just feet from them.

'Did you see anybody 'bout here son?' they asked.

Dumbstruck I turned my head looking down the bank as if to say they went that way and thankfully off they dashed.

You will realise my desperate situation – should I wait until the three ne'er do wells returned; should I leave the salmon and walk away – or even toss it into the river? My head was in a whirl and the afternoon wore on with not a soul appearing. Finally, in a blind panic I decided to walk home with the salmon wrapped in my jacket in the hope that I could think of some way of disposing of it as I went.

But nothing.

'What on earth have you got there?' demanded my mother.

'A fish caught in the river – boys poached it and ran away.'

'What! Show me! Heavens! Your father will go mad if he sees that. You need a licence to take a fish from the river.'

And father did go mad. You see he was precise in everything – scrupulous in the way things were done, and when he saw the salmon, which I had laid out in our bath, the riot act got a fresh airing.

'Don't you realise the bailiffs are friends of mine and I know every fisherman on that river.'

'But we – *you* have a licence,' I protested,

This was true; man and boy he grew up along the river and fished every season. Indeed, I have to say looking into his fishing box was a thrill in itself – copper, orange, yellow and purple flies so beautifully tied it seemed they would come to life any moment.

No wonder then his parting shot – 'I'm going back to work for an hour – it better not be there when I get home – and clean up that bath.'

My protests were lost on him; he was off and I had to think quickly. There was only one thing for it – the beautiful fish would have to disappear from the face of the earth – sad as it was it would have to go under the knife.

I had seen my father clean a fish before so saving readers the gory details suffice to say that in quick time I cleaned out the innards, took off the head and the tail and divided the salmon into half a dozen generous steaks – each of which I wrapped neatly in grease proof paper. Then the *fait accompli* – two steaks put to the side for ourselves and the others I delivered to our good neighbours – four of them. All with the message – 'We got an unexpected delivery today and hope you can accept this little bit left over.'

All of a sudden I went from the naughty boy that kicks football in the street all day to that fine young man from next door.

That evening after tea father pushed his plate to the side empty save for a few fish bones – 'That was a lovely tea mother,' said he. And turning to me continued, 'You made a great job of the bath. Get yourself something.'

So saying he pressed two shillings into my hand and turned away to read his paper and later added – 'By the way I'm getting you a full licence tomorrow.'

Yet, readers will wonder if I ever went back to the river bank? The answer is very little – not because of fear of *Them* – the brothers. You see the oldest went into the army while the other two went to live with their uncle in Wales. As for me, having reached the age of 15 I was eligible to travel with my class for swimming sessions at the city baths.

That was all tightly organised of course – none of the wild excitement of the river bank – no foxes or badgers to spot, no brilliant dive of the orange and blue kingfisher and never again the chance to see the splendour of the magnificent creature that I christened *Silver Flash*.

The Dawning of the Day

I saw the danger and I passed along the enchanted way.
(Patrick Kavanagh)

'We are going to Dublin – we are going to Dublin!' We danced around the living room brother Ben and I as my mother read out the letter from Mrs. Doolin. I was aged seven and he a couple of years older.

All we knew about Dublin was what we had been told; it had escaped the restrictions of war; there would be sweets, pink ice cream and visits to the Botanic Gardens and the Dublin Zoo where Mrs. Doolin's brother was one of the keepers – oh, and of course the train journey. How exciting was that puffing our way for hours from Derry through stations and places we had never heard of.

But to Mrs. Doolin's letter. How it came about is an odd opening to our tale.

My memory creates pictures for me and I can still see the letter in my mind's eye. That is the way with time and me and as you will hear time refused to let go – it would return not so much to haunt but to tell me what it meant.

The letter had come about through a chance meeting of my father and Captain Doolin who had arrived in Derry in his coastal tramp steamer and had called at a local pub. He liked his drink and the two got into conversation; there were tales of adventure in the

China Seas and exotic tropical islands where the conventions of love far exceeded the bounds of Ireland. Then, the next time the captain returned the acquaintance was rekindled and with hospitality at our house the friendship blossomed.

After that came an exchange of letters between my mother and the captain's wife Molly and then the invitation to come to Dublin for a week's holiday – young as I was I remember the Dublin address that when I looked up the map I found was in Drumcondra almost beside the canal and near the famous Croke Park.

While mother was pleased about us getting to Dublin in so much as I was able to read her thoughts I sensed there was something that I just could not put a finger on. As you will hear over the years time would sort that out.

Anyway we got to Dublin's Amiens Street Station all the way from Derry and in grand style took a taxi to the Doolins who lived in a row of small cottage-type houses with the Royal Canal on the other side of the street. Straightaway at the door was Molly Doolin – plumpish and nice looking, with a beautiful soft Galway accent and thrilled to see us – and with a special warm hug for my mother. There too was Captain Roddy Doolin – smug I thought, smoking a pipe and all his welcomes for my father – we boys seemingly no more than accessories.

'The children are playing *Blind Man's Buff* with Katherine – the boys can join them,' said Molly guiding us through an open door to the back yard.

There, amid screams of delight we found Katherine, arms outstretched, with a ribbon round her eyes, in the middle of a circle of three children all trying to dodge her. We sat on a bench to watch as the youngsters, an older boy and two others teased her until eventually one surrendered and the game was over – Katherine then took the ribbon from her eyes.

In that moment my heart skipped a beat for as she discarded the ribbon the older boy took her hand and heavens I realised it was not just *Blind Man's Buff* – really, she was blind.

It absolutely floored me.

'Are these the boys from Derry, Patrick?' she asked, tracing a hand over our faces and then sitting beside us. Patrick was a handsome and polite young man with wavy hair and beautifully spoken like his mother. Soon we were chatting and finding out Katherine was 12, Patrick 11 and the other two a boy of seven and girl of six years whose sight also was not good.

'Come see this,' said Katherine, who was very pretty and mild-mannered; lifting a book as big as a family Bible unto her lap she continued. 'This is my braille primer.'

Some pages had pictures of everyday things and corresponding sets of raised dots and these she was able to read perfectly for me.

'This is nice,' she continued, turning a page, 'it's a beautiful old Irish poem… about a boy who meets a girl and falls in love with her…but it has a sad ending… Then she took my index finger and tracing out the raised dots for me said the words…

> *But she went lonely on her way,*
> *As the morning light was shining bright,*
> *At the dawning of the day.*

'Can *you* imagine, the *dawning* of the day?' I asked awkwardly.

Katherine shook her head. 'I can't, 'said she, 'but I feel it must be wonderful – the coming of light.'

That evening Thaddy Brady from down the row came calling. Small, stooped, stubble faced, and all of 80 years, Molly eased him into the wicker chair by the fire while we children sat on the floor and the grownups sat on settees.

'I just called to see the folk from the North,' said he in a Dublin accent that would have done justice to a Moore Street flower seller. 'Never was there…in the North – but fought along wi' some o'them in the war – Great War – Redmond's boys we were. Did I ever tell ya, Captain?'

'You did Thaddy you did,' replied Captain Doolin dismissively, 'No need now.'

'Ah so,' mumbled the old man, 'but I'll tell ya this, we'll never be short o' wars – an' the China man'll rule the world.'

'A wee dram' said Molly proffering him a glass. 'Now Thaddy, the children are off to see their uncle Jack at the zoo tomorrow – what's the best way for them?'

'Mmm…20 minutes by the side streets…but for the childer let them take the main road to Capel Street then straight to the Liffey an' up past St. Michan's Church – the Phoenix Park – an' the zoo, is ahead o' them. Can't miss Capel Street – rarest sight in Dublin – world o' pawnshops – an' broken hearts. Many a ring was pawned in the poor man's bank.'

At that I saw my mother and Molly glancing at one another yet it meant nothing to me at the time.

So we set out the following day – Katherine, Patrick, Ben and me – each of us boys in turn taking Katherine by the hand and describing the strange old shops in Capel Street before we turned up along the River Liffey. Eventually we found Uncle Jack waiting for us at the zoo entrance.

That day was all wonder for me – the bigness of Dublin – the mood was right and the unbelievable magnificence of the zoo added to the thrill. We were royalty as Uncle Jack took us round everywhere starting with the monkey house 'There are hundreds of monkey breeds,' said he. 'We have Capuchins, Malabars and Macaques, and we don't like folk feeding them.'

The monkeys knew him and he chatted with them seemingly knowing each one. Then to the reptile house where we were permitted to touch a snake – 'Don't worry, 'said Jack; 'he's not poisonous and anyway he sleeps all day long.'

It had a warm, leathery feel. I hated it and I've abhorred snakes ever since but I remember the sad old crocodile would not budge for as us he lay in his pool of water. Finally, to the big lions and tigers – a beautifully striped one recognised Jack and came over to the bars of the cage. 'Don't go near him. Gorgeous as he is he'd eat you in a minute,' Jack added. 'I suppose that's life.'

Then it was a hug for Katherine and a wave for us and off we went again past St Michan's – I noticed an intriguing aroma in the air that Patrick said was from Guinness's Brewery and a funny shaped bridge that he thought was called the Ha'Penny Bridge – Dublin's oldest.

Back at the house my father had gone on a tour of Dublin pubs with the captain, something my mother did not like at all, and while we children were locked into games she and Molly were huddled in conversation. I did not know then but I now realise something that at my young age I did not appreciate – a cloud of sadness hung over that little Dublin family. This perhaps was the subject of Molly's and my mother's intimate chat.

When we got back home the letters between the pair continued but my mother was never one for making judgements, expressing opinions, gossip and the like so little was spoken. Captain Doolin ceased sailing into Derry port and in time the letters stopped too. And so the connection with the Doolins dropped into the background. Only occasionally in later years when my mother was reminiscing came little snippets – nothing direct mind you – Captain Roddy Doolin was not among her favourites. 'And why?' I would ask 'Ah well – least said…' was the usual answer. My guess was that the captain's life – drinking and so on, was not for the modest ways of my father.

Then on another time she hinted about Molly's regrets and for once Molly's side of things got an airing with the story of how she came to meet the captain.

'Far too sore on herself about the outcome,' was mother's view… an innocent girl of 17 years she had met him when he sailed into the little port just outside Galway where she lived. Wandering the quay Molly McGlynn was hailed by the handsome captain with sweet chat, tales of adventure and all the charm of a man who had ploughed the seas across the globe.

Well I suppose a sailor has a girl in every port. Anyway, she fell for him right away – head over heels it was – he, the Pied Piper, she, the star struck devotee.

Love knows no bounds, rides on a wave of bliss; in little time they were married and off she went with him eventually settling in Dublin.

But there was a cost. It was against her parents' wishes and totally so; she had been destined for university, indeed, had even considered a religious vocation in a teaching order of nuns.

All was sacrificed for that is the way of love. But…then there came the children and the pain; Katherine without sight and a younger one whose sight was threatened. She had gone to the hospital consultants who assured her that no blame was to be laid at her door – what was that saying? And was it the case that going home to visit her family for a while in Galway when she got back another woman's touch had been laid on the house – indeed was still there? And the bitter pills of life kept coming for something happened to the wonderful boy Patrick.

I suppose Molly could be forgiven for thinking she had brought a judgement on herself.

As I've explained my mother rarely gave opinions but over the years the pieces of a jigsaw had formed in my mind. I tried not to make conclusions yet the boundaries of the scene were there and whether I liked it or not much of the remainder was coming together. 'Time will explain,' says Jane Austen in *Persuasion* and as you will see somehow time was about to weave its web over me.

It happened in the strangest way. Several decades later we had been visiting my mother's sister in Dublin and upon leaving for home passed close to Drumcondra.

'Do you know we're very near to where the Doolins lived,' said she. 'I'd love to see it again.

Could we…?'

Without giving it much thought I pulled off the highway and believe it or not after a couple of side streets we were outside the door that we had not seen in all those years.

Then typical of my mother she went on, 'I must ask who is living there now.'

Up the little path she went and for an age was engaged in conversation with a woman at the door who eventually appeared to be giving directions. My mother returned beaming – 'Would you believe after all this time Katherine is still about – is married with a boy and a girl and lives just two streets away? We have to see them.'

Excitement was at fever pitch when our knock on the door was answered by a boy of about 19 years who fetched his mother and suddenly there she was – Katherine.

'Oh my goodness!' she burst out. 'Can it be, can it be? How often have we talked about you – the folk from Derry?'

She looked well; late 40s I would say attractive and at ease with herself and despite the shock her welcome was unbounded.

It was an afternoon of recollections and tears but delight as well. Her parents now gone – her mother Molly had been the linchpin of her life and saw her into a happy marriage.

'But father…'

Whatever it was she stopped in her tracks and got back to our long gone visit to the zoo. 'Remember Capel Street – and you hated the snake!'

At that, her memories came flooding back and she turned to me asking, 'Do you recall this?'

So saying she took the large book on the table beside her and you could have knocked me over with a feather at what I saw – it was the braille primer that she had shown me when I was seven years old. Then, as she had done before she took my index finger and traced out the raised dots saying the words…,'

> *But she went lonely on her way,*
> *As the morning light was shining bright,*
> *At the dawning of the day.*

The dawning of the day – the final piece of the jigsaw had fallen into place and I realised there is no escape from the web time throws around us for then is now and now is then.

Note: Poet Patrick Kavanagh has written a haunting version that set to music has become internationally famous:

On Raglan Road of an autumn day
I saw her first and knew,
That I might someday rue.
I saw the danger and I passed
Along the enchanted way.
And I said, "Let grief be a fallen leaf
At the dawning of the day."

The Taming of Kerry Blue

My grandfather was King of Ardmore when he donned his great coat and flat cap and walked out with Kerry Blue. You see Kerry Blue was a wicked terrier – he growled and bared his teeth at everybody – no other dog in the vicinity was safe and it was a standing joke that because of him all the cats in Ardmore had left the country. Mind you that said as a dog he looked magnificent in his beautiful grey blue coat – he was big for his breed and had a strange look in his eyes that was almost human.

No surprise then that grandfather had status when he took to the Ardmore roads. When not on patrol with Kerry Blue he worked in the bleach green down by the River Faughan and at weekends he would go to country fairs with his Rickety Wheel gambling game that earned him a few pounds. So everybody knew him; he was canny too and certainly nobody would cross him especially when Kerry Blue was about.

I should explain that I named him Kerry Blue after the well-known breed but grandfather simply referred to him as *The Dawg*. He was given to him as a pup and no baby got better attention. So the pair became inseparable and with the family grown up, the only other person at their cottage was my lovely granny Elizabeth. However, it came about that my parents decided I should have a few days with them in the country before I started big school; so I was packed off.

Their cottage was a delight – a warm tidy kitchen, flagged floor, a dresser with blue and white plates, bowls and cups and everywhere the homely smell of paraffin from a lamp that was always lit. There was a parlour never used, two bedrooms and a small scullery where larger pots and pans were kept. Out the back there was a small field with a goat, a nice little orchard and outhouses for the hens to lay their eggs and storage for gardening implements,

The cottage was always entered from the back by a driveway along the side and at that end of the dwelling was a water barrel and another barrel on its side that was Kerry Blue's kennel. When not with grandfather he was attached to a chain about 20 feet in length that allowed him to dash out at visitors and scare them to bits. The butcher, the baker and the postman tried to give him a wide berth by tiptoeing as far away from him as possible but it never worked with the result that they were terrified.

All of this I observed upon my arrival at the cottage. Having never met grandfather or indeed Kerry Blue I was very apprehensive for I had heard about the dog's unsavoury reputation. Anyway, grandfather took me out the back on my first day and I stayed my distance while he went over to Kerry Blue who lay on his side while grandfather patted him and tickled his stomach. It was only when the dog noticed me that he sat up and gave a low growl in my direction.

'Calm now boy – it's just our new lodger' said grandfather. At that Kerry Blue obediently rolled over for more tickling before the old man made his way over to me. Tall and wiry he took out his pipe, lit up and continued – 'I *think* you'll be all right…as long as you don't go poking your nose into where it shouldn't be. You see *The Dawg* tells me everything.'

At that Kerry Blue give a bark as if to say – 'Did you hear that?'

'He knows every move. Misses nothing,' added grandfather. 'Do you know he would eat wee boys for his dinner if they misbehaved?'

There was a confirming growl from the dog and a shiver ran down my spine in that moment for I realised loud and clear – Kerry Blue did not like me – and certainly I did not take to him.

Battle lines were drawn and, as I came and went, he would bolt from his barrel towards me as far as his chain would allow and all the while I was planning how I might deal with him for as a new arrival in his patch he was intent in waging war on me.

It was from that time I christened him Kerry Blue. Then I discovered I could unsettle him by using the water barrel for target practice. I became quite good at lobbing pebbles from a distance and at every splash in the water he rushed in my direction – I even hit his barrel deliberately with a nice big pebble and that all but drove him mad.

Yet, as I have told you my grandfather was a canny man and after a few days he came to me – a knowing look in his eye – 'Can you do something for me?' says he. 'I've a notion those rapscallions from up the hill are throwing stones into the water barrel upsetting *The Dawg*. You and I will have to keep watch. We don't want him annoyed – do we?'

His last words were a little forceful so I nodded in agreement – Kerry Blue watching me all the while.

'Now here's the deal,' he went on, taking my hand and placing a shining silver sixpence right in the middle of my palm. 'You keep a look out for those rascals and *The Dawg* and me will deal wi' them. Won't we?' Said he calling over to Kerry Blue who took to barking in agreement.

Grandfather had played his trump card and on evenings after that when he and the dog were leaving for their walk Kerry Blue would look back at me defiantly as if to say – 'You see smart-aleck! You'll not get the better of us.'

What could I do? He had taken to growling at me worse than ever but then one evening I learned how to brave him out by standing a few feet beyond the length of his twenty foot chain. There I could look him straight in the eye and he could bark away to his heart's content.

'You're making him bark too much,' said grandfather.

'I think he'll come round to me in time, Grandpa,' I retorted.

'Aye, in a hundred years maybe, 'he jibed. 'Man, woman, child nor beast – he listens to nobody but me.'

'My teacher said St. Francis could tame animals – even speak to them.'

'If your teacher comes here he'll get a bite in the rump if he's not careful.'

'Still think I might manage it, Grandpa, I may have a way with animals.'

'Have you taken leave of your senses young fella? I'd put a hundred pounds on it he'll only listen to me.'

The very idea that *The Dawg* would listen to anyone other than himself appeared to upset him greatly and I watched as he reached into the pocket of his waistcoat and took out a little purse.

'Tell you what I'll do,' he continued. 'Just to show you how sure I am we'll have a 'wee flutter'. Where's your silver sixpence?'

I produced my sixpence and opening his purse grandfather took out a coin – 'Do you know what this is?' he asked.

The coin had St. George on a horse on one side and Queen Victoria on the other and before I could say anything he went on – 'An 1898 gold sovereign – that's what it is. Now I'll bet my sovereign against your sixpence you'll not get within an inch of that *Dawg*.'

'But… I'd never manage it before I go home at the weekend, Grandpa.'

'Take it or leave it. Today's Wednesday I'll give you to Saturday.'

He polished the coin on his sleeve and I made to have a look at it.

'On no!' said he holding it away from me. 'You'll have to earn it.'

Kerry Blue looked over at me and I knew his growl said 'No chance!'

It came to Thursday and I was still wondering how I might tame him.

Then I remembered seeing him chewing on a bone one day and I went to granny with an idea – 'Is there any chance you would have a bone left over?'

'A bone? What for?

'I want to make friends with the dog.'

'Heavens child only grandfather feeds the dog. I'd have to take to the hills if he found out.'

Yet granny being granny there was a nice juicy bone left out for me on a plate in the scullery.

Kerry Blue did his usual act of charging towards me as far as his chain would allow and I stood a little distance away ready to speak to him; he barking all the while.

'Now, good boy, I have christened you Kerry Blue and if you're nice to me, I'll be nice to you,' said I.

At this he backed away still barking. Holding out the bone I moved towards him and still barking he retreated into his kennel.

My plan was not working but refusing to give up I pulled a little piece of juicy meat from the bone and threw it half-way towards him. Incredibly he came forward collected the meat and ate it with relish. Then I tried the bone again – 'Look Kerry Blue it's for you.'

Stubbornly he made for his kennel again. But then as I turned to leave he gave one single bark. What could it mean – did he want me to stay? As a last resort I placed the bone a little inside the limits of his chain and believe it or not he came up almost as far as me. I could have petted him but was too scared before he collected the bone and made off with it.

The following day was Friday my challenge almost upon me.

Granny had produced another bone 'Not cooked,' she said. 'You don't give a dog cooked bones.'

Then with grandfather at work I set about the same routine as the day before. I showed him the bone, with a juicy piece of raw meat and waited. He did not move but neither did he bark so I stayed on. Ages went by as we stood staring at each other before I pretended to leave. At that he gave another bark and so I tossed meat from the bone towards him as I had done the day before and goodness unbelievably he came right up to me.

Could I? Would I? Dare I?

Closing my eyes I reached out waiting for the crunch of his

teeth – but no. All I felt was the soft hair between his ears so I slowly tickled him. Heart thumping, nervously I eased him over on his side and tickled his stomach as I had seen grandfather doing and Kerry Blue loved it. I was making some ground.

That afternoon I tried again but without any bone or meat yet he stayed by his kennel. At least he did not bark and I decided I was as ready as I could be for the challenge in the morning.

To be truthful I was really anxious about the whole enterprise. Nonetheless the big day arrived.

Placing the gold sovereign and the silver sixpence on the window ledge grandfather called and out came his *Dawg* lively as a spring lamb and allowing himself to be tickled and patted until I thought it would go on all day. But then I noticed something odd – grandfather seemed to whisper something in his ear.

'What was that all about?' I pondered.

'Your go now,' said he, and I took up my station for the challenge.

'Here boy,' I babbled nervously.

But Kerry Blue would not budge as I called over and over again.

My cause was lost and utterly dejected I turned to grandfather only to see he was looking bewildered or appeared to be.

'Well I'm blowed,' said he.

'What is it?' I retorted.

'Look behind you boy.'

I turned to find Kerry Blue sitting looking up at me, tongue out and panting happily away before lying down and practically inviting a tickle. Then within a minute or so he was up and away to his kennel.

I was shocked beyond belief – one moment down, the next triumphant. 'How could it be?'

'Your day,' said grandfather reluctantly proffering me the sovereign and the silver sixpence.

Still amazed I replied -'But I really don't want the sovereign, grandpa.'

'Take it! All's fair in love and war,' he muttered and with no further words off he went with the dog.

I had won, yet had I?

Whatever the case I did not want to upset grandfather so before I left on Sunday I scribbled a note thanking him for a wonderful time and made no mention of victory or defeat. Leaving the note folded over on his bedside table I placed his Queen Victoria sovereign inside it and added a last few words – 'Your dog is the best in the world…'

You may gather I was somewhat hesitant in claiming victory over the taming of Kerry Blue and have been ever since. Why? Well, I have always wondered what grandfather whispered in the dog's ear that day of the challenge – there were no flies on him and I always recall our teacher in school saying- '*There's as much teaching done outside the classroom as inside…*'

Grandfather lived to the ripe old age of 96 years but made no will; however, on an evening not long after he passed away one of the family called with something he had left for me.

When I opened the package what do you think? There before me was the shiny 1898 Queen Victoria gold sovereign and a picture of Kerry Blue.

The Wire

On a fine Saturday in the 1950s Spencer Road is just waking up to the day's business. A narrow, comfortable street, it swings up in a great bend from the River Foyle and straightens out for about another half mile into the heart of Derry's Waterside. It is a street with as many shops as houses; everybody knows everybody – this as the saying goes has been the way forever and a day.

But dear reader today will be different. Folk are still blinking their eyes from sleep but soon something very odd is about to unfold.

Our scene opens as if in one of those old black and white movies – everyone is held in freeze-frame – some about to walk, traffic about to move, even cats and dogs ready to leap into life.

At ten o'clock the day springs into action. On the left just past the bend Mrs. Heaney is washing her front door step and hailing Molly Crawley on the other side of the street about the Sunday Press crossword – 'What did you think about Six Across?'- 'Not sure about it,' laughs Molly. Next door Annie Cheshire is opening the shutters of her tobacco and confectionery shop – they say people come for miles just to savour the beautiful aroma inside – and there across the street are the haircutting brothers John and Harry McClay about to open up; Hunter's Bakery is further along; and on it goes – grocery stores, green grocers, furniture emporiums, pubs and heaven knows what; you could live your life on Spencer Road and never have to go anywhere and many do.

Yet there is one enterprise that does not boast its presence, in fact plays it down; but soon it will be at the centre of our tale on this incredible day – the Bookie's – McGillicutty's Betting Shop to be precise. Around here they call the owner, Matt McGillicutty, a blow-in for he comes from somewhere in the west – nobody knows where that might be and he never goes out of his way to tell them.

His betting shop – a flattering name really, can be found down a dark alleyway that smells of disinfectant, dampness and stale tobacco butts – the latter discarded by punters as they bemoan their losses on the way out.

'It's not exactly Buckingham Palace,' says bookie's clerk Phonsie Kerr to new recruit 15 year-old Seannie Finn – a bright lad willing and able and curious about the inner workings of this odd place.

It's a drab square-shaped room, the floor carpeted in beaten dockets, the walls covered in newspaper racing pages – the only light from a naked bulb hanging by a twisted flex from the ceiling. All day long a Tannoy with a threadbare speaker barks out the start and finish of races in a gravelly voice while at the rear a counter separates the clerk from the punters.

Supervising everything from a tall chair at the very back sits the boss, Matt McGillicutty, his eagle eye missing nothing.

Saturday business is brisk and by mid – morning the place is filled to overflowing – punters studying races at tracks such as Newmarket, York, Kempton Park and Epsom – the air dense with cigarette smoke and you can hardly hear your ears for chatter.

'Lot of dough coming in, Phonsie,' says Seannie.

''Tis son – an'stayin' in.'

'How…?'

'When you're here long enough you'll learn bookies never lose – well…most of the time.'

Phonsie, apart from having a sharp head for calculating, like many in his trade, is a philosopher of human nature, having seen the triumphs, the trials, the ins and outs and the ups and downs that folk forever face in the melting pot of the bookie's shop.

'Ye see Seannie, your bookies is a wee cut o'life in itself. In here they live in Doubles and Trebles and Yankees and heaven knows what. When it gets in the blood men think a fortune's there for the taking – if it's not on this one, it's the next and on they go – see Sammy over there he thinks his system will make him a millionaire – never will. And Barney beside him is afraid to go home to the wife…sometimes she's even at the door outside.'

'Why?'

'Because he's spent the wages – coalman 'ill not be paid this week. Every soul in here has a tale to tell.'

'But Phonsie you know the horses. You could make it.'

'With a wife and five mouths to feed no sir – not for me! Now you get tidying or the boss 'ill be down on ye like a ton o' bricks.

Phonsie is a non-stop smoker, a butt hanging precariously on his lip all day long with the smoke making his eyes blink continually – sometimes, to the amazement of punters he appears to swallow the butt only to reveal it again still lit – off-putting as it is quite often he isn't even aware he is doing it..

Seannie appears at his side – 'Phonsie, old dolls out the front want bets placed.'

'Old dolls – who?'

'One's tall wi' trousers and speaks posh – hair wrapped in a fancy scarf'.

'That's Lilly Verschure from across the street – Dutch. Her father came here during the War. The others?'

'Two the spittin' image of one another.'

'What – the McGinn twins. Surely not?'

The McGinn twins, Jinny and Cassie, are Spencer Road legends. Quiet and petite they dress exactly alike – tan gabardine coats, green felt hats, thick stockings and old-fashioned black patent handbags. They link arms and walk Spencer Road two times a day regular as clockwork.

'Thet're never out o' chapel – can understand them not wanting to darken our door,' mutters Phonsie as he looks at the bets scribbled on scraps of paper – the twins -10 shillings on *Ripe Bananas* ; Lily Verschure – £1… *again* on *Ripe Bananas.*

He frowns for he has a way of keeping track on every race by stacking the docket counterfoils for each runner and *Ripe Bananas* is becoming far the largest.

Seannie arrives with more bets for the same mount – 'Half o' Spencer Road's out there. Queue's a mile long an'they're complaining they won't get a bet on before the race.

Phonsie turns to look up at McGillycutty – 'Boss, something's cooking.'

'What?'

' Kempton Park, three o'clock – ten furlong – a runner called *Ripe Bananas.*'

'Ripe Bananas – never heard of it.*'*

'Me neither but it's spreading like wildfire – the whole of Spencer Road's going for it.'

'Price Phonsie – price?'

'Fifty-to-one.'

McGillycutty almost falls off his chair. 'A *wire* – must be! Knew something was going to happen this day. Better check it out! You boy! What's your name?'

'Seannie, sir – Mr. McGillycutty.'

'Get out into Spencer Road and find what's going on – where's it coming from.'

'But what's a *wire*?'

'A *wire's* a message from a stable that they're going to run a horse that's been brought on to make a big challenge in a race.

Seannie is back in minutes gasping – 'Oul Sadie Campsie at the top of the road got a phone call from somebody called Tiny!'

'Tiny Campsie! That's her grandson,' adds Phonsie. 'He wasn't the size of sixpence and went to train as a jockey at a stable in England. Came home last year driving a Jaguar as long as a street.'

'The whole street will be driving Jaguars if we don't sort this out,' snaps McGillicutty. It's a wonder we've never heard of that horse. Give me the form book Phonsie. '

McGillycutty scans the book but finds nothing.

'You know I'm surprised Sadie Campsie could handle a phone call, 'says Phonsie. She's been deaf for donkey's years.'

'What's in the field ?' McGillicutty asks.

'*Charming girl, Cricklewood Lad, the Gent and Sea Shanty* evens, with *Misty Wood* 7 to 4, *Striped Pyjamas* 20 to 1… and *Ripe Bananas* 50 to 1.'

'What did you say – *Striped Pyjamas…Ripe Bananas?*' And you tell the old woman's deaf?'

'Deaf as a post she is.

'*Striped Pyjamas…Ripe Bananas…* 'McGillycutty keeps repeating. 'What is it Boss?'

'I'm beginning to see, Phonsie… yes siree, I'm beginning to see. The names of those two runners nearly sound the same. Being deaf she's taken *Ripe Bananas* when really it should have been *Striped Pyjamas!* Your Spencer Road punters are barking up the wrong tree! We're in clover!'

'You think she's mixed it up. The *wire* was really for *Striped Pyjamas?*'

'Sure of it. *Ripe Bananas* is probably ready for the knackers yard!'

'Hope you're right, Boss. But…maybe play it safe.'

'No way! It's my hunch and just to show how certain I am I'm going to lay money on *Striped Pyjamas* – 50 quid across the other two bookies in town – 25 pounds straight on each.'

Shaking his head Phonsie telephones to lay the money off and the time wears up to three o'clock.

'Off at Kempton,' barks the Tannoy.

Suddenly the whole place falls silent; many in the room have heard about the *Wire* and have risked a flutter as on comes the Tannoy again. 'And it's level going at the bend…now *Cricklewood Lad*'s ahead of *Charming Girl,* The *Gent* and *Sea Shanty* …it's steady going at the five furlong marker… but *Striped Pyjamas* is making ground as they go to the final bend…*Cricklewood Lad* and *The Gent* still ahead of the field…but *Striped Pyjamas* is now level… and coming up on the outside and gaining ground it's *Ripe Bananas* . . .

it's neck and neck with *Striped Pyjamas and Ripe Bananas . . . Ripe Bananas* moves ahead – it's *Ripe Bananas* – *Ripe Bananas* wins! Outsider takes it!

McGillicutty's Bookies erupts – cheering, papers flung in the air, handshakes and backslaps and on Spencer Road it is like a fair day. Everybody out-of-doors; delight and smiles all round – money made – nothing like it ever seen. They may not be millionaires but as the saying goes in Waterside it's *fish and chips* for supper tonight.

'What have I done?' says McGillicutty, head in hands, as Phonsie pays the unending stream of punters. 'What are we down?'

'Other side of a Grand?' replies Phonsie. 'And there's also the 50 pounds you laid off.'

'Phonsie, what's a Grand,?' asks Seannie.

'Son, it's hardly the time for questions but if you must know it's a thousand pounds.'

'Wow, that's hard on the Boss.'

'Don't concern yourself,' whispers Phonsie. 'He'll make it up in a week,'

Yet the Boss is licking his wounds – 'It's a disaster. I'll know to listen to you next time Phonsie. Anyway, I need to clear my head – you lock up and if I ever hear the word *wire* again I'll take to the hills.'

As Phonsie turns the key he smiles and says to Seannie – 'You've had a tough baptism young fella.'

'Enjoyed it – and I've a little something for you.'

So saying he thrusts a crisp white 10 Pound Note into Phonsie's hand.

'What in the name of heaven…!' Declares Phonsie.

'I had a little flutter myself from the tips I got for placing bets for the folks outside – not bad for a beginner.'

'You *are* learning fast! Anyway, never look a gift horse in the mouth so I'll take it – and thanks!'

Seannie quips – 'And when you're passing Anderson's greengrocers get something for the family.'

'What would you be thinking?'

'I'd be thinking...umm...why not some *ripe bananas!*' says Seannie skipping off with an impish giggle.

How Many Miles to Babylon?

Can I get there by candle-light?
(Traditional Poem)

On their favourite walk by the river it is not a good day for Jamie and Alessia – both are 18 years of age and are gripped by the burning desire to share life together but…the road before them is a rocky one.

'Look Alessia, if we want to get married just let's do it.'

'But if your grandfather and my parents are against it…?'

'We've been over it again and again. Alessia, it's about us. How many times have we heard we're too young? Please say you'll agree.'

'I do, but with you still a student, there's just the income from my part-time work in the bookshop. How shall we manage?'

'We shall somehow. I'll break it to grandfather this evening.'

With his mother dying when he was an infant and his father a few years back Jamie, who has been brought up with his grandfather Daniel Cullen, attends art classes at college. As yet his efforts to sell paintings have not been a success – only Mr. Jacobs of the art shop has taken one of his works for display. No surprise then that tempers are already frayed about his future. Also, Daniel has heard rumours about Jamie and Alessia; nonetheless to get the news from his grandson in such a blunt way that evening riles him beyond measure.

'Marriage! What's this nonsense?'

Daniel will have none of it. A stonemason by trade, highly skilled and respected he is as old-fashioned as they come – everything done by the book, his motto being that there is a time and place for everything and a boy of 18 years of age marrying fits nowhere into his view of life.

'Let me tell you something young man love might warm your bed but it won't pay the bills. If you go ahead with it as I think you intend to then that's the end of all between us. You can no longer stay here nor will the attic be available as your studio.'

He loves Jamie like a son, nonetheless closing his mind to sentiment, he continues with bitter parting words, 'That's all I have to say. Pack your bags as suits. As for your art it's all mumbo jumbo to me!'

Later a despondent Jamie meets up with Alessia who reveals she has taken her mother into her confidence. 'Mother's not for it either but she won't stand in my way and I think she'll soften the blow with father.'

'I feel bad about hurting grandfather', sighs Jamie. 'And would you believe he more or less said my art was rubbish. Alessia, I want people to see and feel things in my colours, shapes and designs – not pictures of thatched cottages – no one understands.'

Yet Alessia as usual is warm with her words – 'I'll support you every step of the way until you're famous,' she tells him even though the girl herself is not a little mystified by his abstract art.

And so she eases his misery. Alessia is named after her father's Italian mother – a tradition in Italy, the family having fled troubles there two generations back. She is dark-eyed and olive skinned with just a suspicion of pink on her cheeks and no wonder she captivated Jamie on their first encounter. Those dark eyes had a conversation of their own that spoke of a vivacious nature, tenderness and something else that sprang into life – the inexplicable emotion that besets two souls and binds them into one when Cupid shoots his arrow.

It happened when they first set eyes upon one another. That for which there is no antidote – nor did Jamie want one for never had such a feeling overwhelmed him before – his shyness melted away, his likeable nature and pleasant youthful charm blossomed forth and reaching into Alessia's heart it engendered between them that sensation of bliss called love – love as ever love could be.

'In olden times we'd just have run away together and made the best of it. ' continues Jamie. 'Let's see the priest tomorrow.'

And this they do.

Father Devitt, the parish priest, furrows his brows. Instinctively knows what is afoot when they present themselves at his door. He had heard of young folk like this wanting to marry but it had never occurred with him personally.

'I take it you are here to have the banns announced,' says he.' You know they must be read out at least three weeks before hand.

Jamie and Allesia look at one another in shock, 'But we want to get married right away – we've told our folks.' stammers Jamie.

'Well I'm afraid you can't,' replies the priest. 'Do you *have* to get married so quickly?'

Jamie blushes – is speechless, and Alessia knowing what he means shakes her head.

There is silence. But then the priest goes to his bookcase and flicking through a volume continues – 'Not that I condone it for a minute but under extreme circumstances if you absolutely insist – demand, I see that I may carry out a *Sacristy Marriage* – not in the body of the church and not with Holy Mass. I shall say no more. Present yourselves tomorrow morning at seven o'clock – my housekeepers will serve as witnesses. A wedding ring is not necessary but preferable.'

Shaking his head he goes off to fix the necessary papers and for Jamie and Alessia it is a mixture of relief on the one hand but nervousness bordering on panic on the other. Then, come the following morning, with the streets deserted, both arrive at the appointed hour for the ceremony. With little spoken Jamie and Alessia young as they are become man and wife within minutes. However, it is not time for the joys of marital union just yet for keeping their marriage a secret they must remain at their homes for a few days more until a room is secured.

Alessia prays her mother stays on her side as she gathers her bits and pieces together while Jamie does likewise including his precious mahogany easel that his father had bought for him to encourage his interest in painting – 'Your picture is part of many things – your paints, canvass, brushes and most certainly your easel.' were his father's words and he would never forget them.

As for Alessia's mother despite the unbelievable sadness, she agrees not to break it to the family until Alessia has slipped away. Taking the girl's hand she passes her a gorgeous shell cameo – oval shaped with a white carved classical head on a soft pink background and bordered in gold. Continuing she says – 'This cameo has been handed down from your great-grandfather who lived in Florence and worked in a studio making precious objects on the Ponte Vecchio, the famous bridge over the River Arno. It was made by his hand and is very dear to us.'

It takes a week before they find a cheap room in a squalid part of town – no luxuries – a sofa, a table and two chairs and a brass bedstead just about hanging together; miserable cooking and bathroom facilities are to be shared.

Alessia's family are stunned at the news she has married – Jamie's grandfather is incredibly hurt but, slave to his resolute ways, dismisses it from his mind.

For the young couple finally to be together on their own terms and wrapped in each other's arms there is no feeling to describe it. Bliss does not recognise squalor – peeling wallpaper, mould, drafts nor creaking floorboards. Occasionally, Alessia takes out the cameo and Jamie holds it against her saying – 'It's so charming but you really need to be able to wear it round your neck on a gold chain.'

What chance of that given their dire poverty?

Drawn together as they are all that matters is togetherness – she part of him he of her. The only urge is to please each other 'What can I do to show Jamie how much I love him?' is uppermost in

Alessia's mind, the same in Jamie's for Alessia.

Cupid is beaming but on a cautionary note he is known to be mischievous as he presides over the ecstasies of lovers.

It happens that after they have gone to bed of an evening Alessia asks Jamie, 'Why aren't you painting these days?'

'I've no money to buy paints,' he replies playing it down and the incident appears to be forgotten.

Yet, as days roll by the preoccupation to please one another is ever present until one afternoon fate, which of course has already been spinning its web around them, raises its head all the more.

Now dear reader if the great writer Homer is to be believed fate is waiting in the wings for all of us from the day we are born – who we are and what we are rules our existence determining the consequences of our lives and of course that is the case for our two young lovers.

So it is that down a dingy little alley off the town square Alessia finds herself outside premises, which state in faded gold writing – *Noah Blake Pawnbroker*. It has all the look of a rundown shop – the bow widow with its bulls eye glass panes tips so far out it must surely topple onto the pavement one day. On display Alessia can see jewellery, watches, gold rings and ornaments and pushing the door open, to the jangle of a bell, she is greeted by Noah himself – 'Do come in,'

What confronts her eyes in the pale gas light is a mass of jumble – piles of clothes, hats, umbrellas, dozens of ticking clocks and submerged in the middle of it all is Noah sitting at a stout oak counter. Behind him on several shelves are brown paper packages all labelled with peoples' names.

A sign reads: Pledges to be Redeemed in 27 days – Otherwise Sold.

'Now young lady,' says Noah in an accent that is not local, 'what can I do for you?'

Meanwhile, back at their room Jamie taking advantage of Alessia's absence collects his canvass, brushes and easel and makes off. And is it not a strange twist that Jamie is now bound for the town square and the dingy alley that just a short time ago saw Alessia gaze into the window of *Noah Blake Pawnbroker*? Indeed only minutes separate them encountering one another.

'Now young man,' says Noah, 'what can I do for you?'

That evening both the young folk are in buoyant mood. 'Alessia, I have a surprise for you,' smiles Jamie.

'And would you believe Jamie that I have something for you?'

'Really?' he responds not a little taken aback. 'Well then – let's not look but put what we have for each other on the bed and then open our eyes together.'

This they do eyes tight shut.

'Now!' calls Jamie.

Oh Cupid prince of gods and men what have you done?

Heartbreak! Heartbreak! Heartbreak!

From each a cry of disbelief – then anguish.

There before them are five tubes of paint Alessia has purchased from the pawning of her cameo and beside them a dazzling gold chain Jamie has purchased from the pawning of his brushes, canvass and easel.

Alessia holds the chain letting it fall softly into her hand but there is no cameo for it now. Jamie lifts the tubes of paint – titanium white, burnt sienna, cadmium red and yellow, and Prussian blue – the poet Wordsworth's favourite colour. Yet what good are they with his painting things gone.

All they can do is hold one another and weep bitterly. Suddenly, with bliss banished, the room is nothing but squalor and smelling of mould – the bottom fallen out of their world. Such are their tears that they do not hear the first tap on the door before Jamie at last moves to open it.

Who can it be?

The lad cannot believe his eyes for unbelievably out of the blue it is his grandfather who does not need a second look to see disaster has overtaken the two tear-stained young people before him. Daniel

Cullen listens as their story unfolds – each to show their love for one another have pawned that most precious to them.

'Noah Blake, you say,' the old man goes on. 'I've done a favour or two for him in my time. We'll see to that all right.'

The pair are dumbstruck.

Grandfather continues – 'Now you may be wondering what brings me here? Well…I've been thinking living alone in that big house of mine it's time it had some life about it. Take some of the rooms for yourself and I've done up the attic studio for you already Jamie. I must say you've chosen a stunning girl.'

He did not say if he had been keeping an eye on them, or if he had heard of their plight or indeed if Noah Blake had been in touch with him. However, they say stonemasons have nothing to learn.

On mid-winter days when the rain lashes down and the earth is grey sometimes the clouds forget themselves and let a sliver of sunlight through that beams its way on to the land returning it to all its glory – such it is for Jamie and Alessia.

Grandfather has not finished – 'Oh, I almost forgot. Jacobs the art shop man called to say he had some good news for you. Get in touch with him. You know I always knew you'd make it.'

Cameos

The Honeymoon Tree

Just outside Ballybofey in County Donegal in the overgrown garden of the Conyngham family home one finds a most wonderful reminder of love in Victorian times – the *Honeymoon Tree*. Sometimes called the *Matrimonial Tree* this true curiosity is a very rare sight and at first glance resembles a large tree with an archway running through it. Closer inspection shows that it is really two trees grown into one. The tradition was that when an engagement was announced two saplings were planted side by side. Then when the wedding took place the saplings would be grafted so that the trees grow joined together – the appearance being of two trees lower down that grow up into one. While only one good specimen now remains in the garden there are broken and fallen remnants of others eerie and ghost like – reminders of trysts, love affairs and who knows what of days long gone.

[from *Following the Foyle* 2008]

Rudyard Kipling in Derry

In Derry City Cemetery, believe it or not, written on a gravestone is the name Rudyard Kipling. No, the great writer is not buried here but odd to relate the Rudyard Kipling mentioned on the stone was a relation of his. He was the son of Dudley Kipling, a London man who came to Derry to manage Welch and Margetson's shirt factory on Carlisle Road in 1942. Kipling had three sons and a daughter and became a very popular manager. Derry was much to his liking and he eventually settled in the Waterside. His second son named Dudley Rudyard became a cadet and eventually was to serve in Burma against the Japanese – one of World War II's most vicious campaigns. The boy was the apple of his father's eye and he christened him Rudyard after his famous ancestor.

Sadly, Rudyard was killed on the last day of the war in Burma (5 April1945). The death broke his father's heart as factory workers recalled. Yet it was not the end of grief for the family – in 1949 Dudley lost his daughter at the age of 22 and then tragedy struck Dudley himself. He was travelling back from London to Derry on the ill-fated *Princess Victoria* via the Stranraer to Larne crossing on January 31st, 1953 when the vessel perished in a massive storm with the loss of 133 lives. Dudley's body was recovered and on the way to the city cemetery for burial the cortege paused at the Welch Margetson factory to a large outpouring of grief from all the workers.

The story of young Rudyard Kipling came to light in an odd way. Derry engineer Stanley Page working in Yangon (Formerly Rangoon, Burma) while visiting the Taukkyan War Cemetery there was astonished to see Rudyard Kipling's name listed under his family in Londonderry and buried in Plot 20.B.16.(of the Yangon cemetery).

Thus in the most peculiar of ways young Rudyard Kipling's name appears on two grave stones thousands of miles apart Yangon and Derry. Life can be strange.

The Mysterious Lady of Boom Hall

Boomhall, which takes its name from the boom across the River Foyle during the siege of 1689 is located on the left bank of the river close to the Foyle Bridge. Now a ruin, it dates to c.1779 and was the home of the distinguished Alexander family until the 1840s. Significantly, the Rev.Robert Alexander born in Boomhall was the father of William, Protestant Bishop of Derry and Raphoe, and later Protestant Primate of Ireland (1896-1911). He was regarded as one of the leading orators of his day.

Among many yarns about Boom Hall William Alexander's Memoir contains the interesting tale of a mysterious lady who was discovered wandering very distressed in the grounds of the dwelling close to the bank of the river. She was in tears, beautifully dressed, and refused to speak. The Alexanders, a benevolent family, took her in for safety and when it became evident that she had nowhere to go decided to give her shelter until her plight could be resolved. She insisted on working for her keep and indicated that she would like to be 'below stairs' with the servants, assisting with laundering, ironing needle work, and repairs. It was not long before the Alexanders discovered that she was brilliant at dressmaking. Also it turned out that she was very good with the Alexander children who would visit her and she made a beautiful bedspread for young John Alexander (later, William's father). Yet she never spoke.

Then one day Mrs Alexander heard the most awful commotion coming from below stairs. A row had broken out among the servants and somehow the mysterious lady had got drawn into it. Mrs Alexander descended the stairs quickly only to behold the lady babbling in a language she had never heard of while the shocked servants looked on. Predictably, it all ended in tears until Mrs. Alexander brought calm to the situation. Strangely, thereafter the lady would speak in a language no one in the house or indeed in Derry could understand. She became a well-loved member of the family and in time passed away being buried privately.

The riddle of the mysterious lady and her strange tongue was never solved. One suggestion was that she had been on a Portuguese ship that came into Derry and having committed some misdemeanour upon leaving port on the way down river she had been put off the vessel at Boomhall.

The only evidence that she had ever stopped with the Alexanders was her gorgeous dress and magnificent bedspread that she had made for young John Alexander – prized family souvenirs.

Good Morning Your Reverence…!

Jack Bell sees the light

Jack Bell's smithy was on the left side of the road a little before the hill that takes one down to Fahan in County Donegal. Therein man and boy Jack learned the skills of working with iron and dealing with horses needing to be shod. His smithy was chock-full of iron – gates, frames, flat strips and inevitably piles of horseshoes. When he stirred the cinders and put the bellows on his fire the whole room would light up with a red and orange glow and it was fascinating to see him take a humble piece of iron and forge it into a horseshoe. Then an absolute thrill as he trimmed a hoof and fitted a shoe with the horse obediently allowing its hock to sit between his knees.

'Never stand behind a horse,' he would warn me, still chatting away as he went about his work.

'I've had a bit of a to-do,' says he to me one day. 'We've a new Canon at the chapel.'

'Oh,' says I knowing Jack was a witty old-fashioned country philosopher.

'First Monday he arrived he came walking past the front here his eyes deep in his prayer book. "Good morning Your Reverence," says I, but glued to his book not a word did he speak. That is a very religious man, I thought.'

'Then what, Jack?'

'Would you believe the very same thing happened the Tuesday, Wednesday and Thursday – I saying – "Good morning Your Reverence," and him not paying a wit to me. I thought to myself he's either deaf or bound straight for heaven…or maybe the smithy's not grand enough? So the Friday morning I was ready for him and well steamed up.'

'Don't tell me Jack!'

'Oh Yes! "Good morning Your Reverence," says I. "Ye bl…y oul b…!'

'Oh Good morning, Jack,' says he with a smile, 'isn't that a lovely day!'

The Mystery of the Dead Boy on a Dolphin

The breath taking sculpture *Dead Boy on A Dolphin* is renowned as one of the finest works of art to come out of Italy in the 1700s. Done in white marble it depicts a young boy on the back of a dolphin – the legend originally attributed to the Roman poet Aelianus recounts how a boy befriended a dolphin and the pair had wonderful times enjoying the sea until the youngster got accidentally wounded on the creature's dorsal fin and died. Grief stricken the dolphin managed to get the boy to the shore and died beside him.

There is a mystery to this magnificent piece and a local connection too.

Firstly,the original work is frequently attributed to Raphael in error for it turns out that Lorenzo Lorenzetti (1490-1541) made the original sculpture probably based on a Raphael drawing. Then in the 1700s Nollekens a sculptor of Dutch parentage made at least two stunning reproductions based on a copy made by the renowned sculptor Cavaceppi.

The exciting thing is that one of the Nollekens sculptures made its way into the art collection of Frederick Hervey, the Earl Bishop, at Downhill. It is believed that Hervey purchased it in Rome in the late 1760s. The fame of the Nollekens' work is shown by the fact that the other copy is in the world famous Hermitage museum in St. Petersburg, Russia.

It was not known that the Earl Bishop had purchased *Dead Boy on a Dolphin* and it only came to light when the catalogue for the Great Exhibition in Dublin was published in 1853. Sir Henry Hervey Bruce (3rd Bart) of Downhill is listed as lending it to the Exhibition. Visitors between May and October – even Queen Victoria – would have viewed it.

Thereafter, it vanished again only to appear at Ickworth House,

Suffolk. One must presume that when the Bruces left Downhill in the 1920s they presented the sculpture along with several of Hervey's treasures including old master paintings to Ickworth, the Earl Bishop's ancestral home. He had cut his family out of all his possessions in his will so they went to the Bruces, his relatives. So, a debt resettled perhaps?

The sculpture *Dead Boy on A Dolphin* formerly at Dowbhill would be worth a fortune in today's world.

Derry's Legendary Ballerina

What a puzzle it is that more prominence is not given to one of the most outstanding ballet dancers of modern times Derry girl Ailne Phillips. Born in the city in 1905 and taking ballet lessons from infancy, she first began to dance professionally in the Carl Rosa Opera Company, which was directed and owned by her father the famous impresario H.B. Phillips. No doubt her mother the concert pianist Annette Philips (formerly Netty Prior of Ferryquay Street) helped shaped her dancing.

Ailne or 'Babs' as she was popularly known was one of six dancers who formed the original Sadler's Wells Ballet, which then became the Royal Ballet, she being a founder member. Apart from occasional appearances for other companies Ailne also worked again for the Carl Rosa and finally became one of the top teachers in the world-class Royal Ballet School. It was here that she met the famous Ninette de Valois doyen of modern ballet. They became bosom friends and through performances and teaching they shaped ballet right into today's world.

Babs was popular across the whole performance scene. Described as lovable and charming it seems her vivacious personality touched all those who knew her. Derry can be justly proud of this outstanding girl. A plaque alongside those of Charlie Chaplin, Gracie Fields, Laurence Oliver and many other great names, is dedicated to her parents HB and Netty Philips in St. Paul's, the *Actors Church* in Covent Garden – would it not be fitting that a suitable honour might be made in Derry to mark this great dancer?

Ailne died in 1992. Among her epitaphs – one newspaper quoted a prominent ballet manger's feelings – 'She was the kindest of people, kind to me, kind to us all. What Babs Phillips and de Valois introduced is what ballet is today.'

Ailne Phillips, dancer and teacher, born Derry/Londonderry, 5 June 1905, died Hove (Brighton) 5 October 1992.

Derry Hosts a Famous Ship… and, a Medal for a Cat!

Back in 1954 a buzz of excitement went round Derry with the news that the famous ship *HMS Amethyst* was to be 'mothballed' at Lisahally as part of the Navy's Reserve Fleet. Derry at the time was still a hub for the defence of the Atlantic.

Amethyst, a frigate, made world news in 1949 with a daring escape from the Yangtze River after heavy bombardment by Chinese artillery. Forty-six men died and dozens were injured, but oddly, one of the great heroes of the incident was the ship's cat Simon.

The vessel was a star attraction at Lishally and one worker recalled: 'I remember being in her radio room – no bigger than a cupboard – hardly damaged, it was filled with the equipment that signalled the news of the Chinese attack to the world with loss of life and the captain's cabin destroyed.'

Yet it was the captain's cabin where the truly remarkable story of the ship's cat unfolded. The black and white tom cat had been found in Hong Kong by the captain and taken on board to the delight of the crew.

It was named Simon and soon became a friend to everyone – except the rats, which plagued the ship. However, on that fateful day on the Yangtze in April 1949, when the Chinese fired on the Amethyst, Simon was curled up asleep in the captain's cabin. Suddenly, a direct hit blew a 15" hole in the bulkhead and left him buried under a heap of twisted metalwork. The crew were devastated – shipmates lying dead all around, mayhem everywhere and their pet cat lost. It could only mean a doomed mission. But Simon had other ideas. Battered and bruised, and no doubt drawing on all his nine lives, he managed to free himself. As if out of nowhere, he appeared again to the utter astonishment and delight of the remaining personnel. Thereafter, he was given the title of *Able Seaman Simon*.

Eventually, when medals were to be presented to the crew for bravery they insisted Simon be included. As a result he was awarded the *Dickin Medal for Gallantry* – the only cat ever to receive such an accolade. Shortly afterwards a special collar was sent for Simon to wear yet there was to be a heartrending end to the story for while preparations were being made for his medal presentation Simon suddenly fell ill and died from heart failure. Truckloads of cards, letters and flowers arrived at where he was being cared for and there was even a photograph and tribute to Simon in Time magazine.

Of course, Simon was long gone by the time *Amethyst* arrived in Derry in 1954. But where was his medal? Patrick Roberts, a writer on cats who took an interest in Simon believes the medal might well have been on board the vessel at Lisahally. Later, it came into the hands of a private dealer and amazingly was sold for £23,000 in 1993. Simon is buried in the animal cemetery at Ilford outside London and the story of *Amethyst* was made into a movie in 1957 – the *Yangtse Incident* starring Richard Todd.

Can it be Believed?

The Best Man Marries the Bride!

Not far from Derry in a little village in County Tyrone in 1937 a most extraordinary wedding took place – believe it or not the best man was accidentally married to the bride. It was to be a small private affair but once the newspapers got hold of it and the story went viral across the world even to Australia.

The wedding was to take place with just the bride and groom and a couple of witnesses. However, the groom was very nervous before hand and he and he best man got together to calm their nerves with a little tipple. The 'little tipple' became drink after drink until it appears the pair had to rush to the church 'three sheets to the wind' as the saying goes. In the end everyone was panicking and when the minister put the question – '*Do you take this woman to be your wife?*' the best man, who was closer to the bride than the groom, in his confused state answered 'Yes!' 'Then I pronounce you man and wife,' said the minister.

It was only when they moved into the vestry to sign the registry that the minister to his horror discovered that the groom, who had been silent all the while, had played no part in the ceremony. Thinking quickly on his feet the minister rushed the bride and the groom to the altar and quickly married them – the bride exercising supreme composure.

When the news got out the question on everyone's lips was – 'Were the first pair really married?'

If so should some sort of dissolution have taken place before the proper marriage?

In the event it all settled down and it's said that the little Tyrone village was the only place on earth where the bride was married to two different men inside the space of half an hour.

Buckie O'Boyle's Gold

I am reliably informed by my relative, the renowned Donegal boat builder Michael O'Boyle, that we are descended from a well-known sea captain and pilot also called Michael O'Boyle who plied his trade in the early 1800s. He was called Buckie after a Scottish seaman nicknamed Buckie who was famous for his heroic deeds in rescuing ships in peril during fierce storms.

The O'Boyles hailed from Rutland Island, which is situated about half a mile from Burtonport Harbour in the parish of The Rosses in West Donegal. It happened that in the maze of islands thereabouts a Portuguese barque carrying a valuable cargo got into difficulties in a storm growing into gale force. The master had put down his anchors fore and aft to avoid drifting onto the rocks but it was clear he would lose the battle as the storm increased. Aware of the crisis with the waves now mountainous the coastguard sent word to Captain Michael (Buckie) O'Boyle asking what might be done for the plight of the vessel.

Surveying the scene O'Boyle felt if he managed to get on board he could pilot it to safety. It called for absolute bravery so, taking a rowing skiff 23 feet long and four of his best men he transported the boat six miles across the land to a beach within sight of the stricken vessel. Then during a drop in the wind they pushed their rowing boat out into the angry seas. It was hazardous – the stuff of heroes and not without a few perilous moments until they managed to board the barque.

Of course it was not over but O'Boyle knew every twist and turn of the tides around the islands off Burtonport so there was none better for the task. Yet before he allowed the crew to weigh the fore and aft anchors Buckie said to the Captain – 'Master, the wind will take you on to the rocks where the vessel will not be salvageable or I can pilot you to safety – but for that you must pay the cost for such a risky undertaking.'

'And what is that?' asked the master.

Taking off his peaked cap Buckie continued, 'You or your owners must guarantee to give me gold sovereigns that will fill the space of the bottom of this cap.'

The master had no choice and hurriedly signed an undertaking to pay Buckie who in the teeth of the tempest successfully made it into Burtonport and a hero's welcome. Yet as it turned out the owners of the barque tried to renege on the undertaking and only a court case and coastguard evidence won the day for Buckie in what came to be known as *Buckie's Gold*.

How much space was at the bottom of Buckie's cap? If it could have been covered by 50 or 60 soverigns it was a fortune even after Buckie paid his men. These days an 1820 pure gold sovereign is worth £800.

A Whiskey Man's Fate

Died in Barnesmore Mountain, County Donegal
James McMinimen, generally known as the Buck of Barnes.
His death was occasioned by his drinking for a wager,
three quarts and a pint and a half of strong whiskey. |
Some of our modern bucks, who have occasionally
visited his mansion, have reason to remember the
warmth of his hospitality.
The Londonderry Journal (1791)

The Local Hero Who Travelled the Arctic Wastes

*The Arctic trails have their secret tales that
would make your blood run cold…*
(Robert Service)

In the first decade of the 1900s on the Waterside's Clooney Terrace there were no more popular lads than the Conn brothers Hugh and William – helpful and charming is the way they were described. Of rural stock from the townland of Claggan near Limavady the Conns had come into Derry to set up a grocery business. Not long before, in the absence of work, their uncle had travelled to Canada to seek out possibilities in the famous Hudson Bay Company that traded in fur worldwide. The company covered a large part of the territory on the eastern seaboard of Canada.

News coming back was so good that in 1911 the Conn brothers decided to sell up and travel to Canada with their mother. Hugh was offered a post in the Hudson Bay's Winnipeg sales shop and so impressed his employers he was transferred to the Fur Trade Department in Ontario. From then after training in Arctic conditions with canoes, snow shoes, sleds and dogs his rise was meteoric. He would travel the length and breadth of the Arctic lands organising the collection of fur.

Promoted to general inspector of the Fur Trade his temperament seemed suited to the lonely barren snow covered wastes where his only company was his dogs and outposts of Inuits (formerly known as Eskimos). He even travelled as far as the Arctic Circle, his diaries showing the hazards he encountered – on one occasion during a storm with his dogs covered in snow and asleep he was obliged to keep awake over days and nights for fear of hypothermia.

All the while Hugh Conn was becoming a legend in Canada; he had an interest on the lost Franklin Expedition (1845) and was able to travel the reverse North Passage (West to East) this the opposite of what Franklin was trying to achieve. Of great interest is that almost 80 years later through the Inuits he was able to find some of the remains of the ill-fated Franklin expedition including part of a sextant.

In all the Hudson Bay Company reckoned that Hugh Conn travelled at least 60,000 miles in pursuit of his duties. He had walked hundreds of miles in snow shoes, canoed rivers and travelled thousands of miles over ice and snow with his beloved dogs. His dedication, skills and charm made Hugh Conn a much-loved man. Of course the folk of the Waterside had noticed this trait in the Conn lads many years before.

In the end his 23 years in the Arctic wastes took their toll and he was forced to retire in 1933. Yet Hugh had never forgotten his home land. He travelled back to Ireland and Claggan where he lived quietly and modestly for the next 20 odd years shrugging off all the fame he had achieved both in the Hudson Bay Company and as a great legend in Canada itself. He died in 1963 and is buried at Ballykelly.

The Loneliness Stone

Just a few miles past Kilmacrenan in County Donegal in beautiful wooded and hilly country one finds Churchill – a hallowed place with a feel of ancient Ireland about it. No small wonder for this is the land of Columcille where a flat irregular stone is said to be the birthplace of the saint. Others say St. Columba slept on this stone to ease his grief before he exiled himself to Iona.

It olden days it was known as *Leac na Cumba* the *Flagstone of Loneliness* or the *Flagstone of Grief.*

These days it is simply called the *Loneliness Stone.*

Whether Columba was born here or slept here the stone itself has taken on a mystical significance. Some believe lying on it relieves grief, others say it has healing powers and still others feel it eases loneliness and loss.

As a result in the great exodus or diaspora of people from Ireland in past centuries many emigrants slept on the stone before making the trip into Derry to make passage for America. Accounts talk of the stone wet with tears and glistening in the moonlight – this part of a long tradition before the hazards of the Atlantic crossing.

In less romantic terms geologically the stone is thought to be part of a megalithic tomb. It is covered with small cup-marks and also stained from coins left by those making a wish.

But for emigrants and the broken-hearted it will always be the *Loneliness Stone.*

Develop a Limp

In the 1930s and 40s Sir Ian Fraser of the Royal Victoria Hospital Belfast was one of the country's most eminent surgeons and President of the Royal College of Surgeons based in Dublin. His father was a doctor and his mother Alice was the daughter of Doctor Cuthbert of Gortfoyle House in Derry's Waterside.

Apart from being a renowned surgeon Sir Ian had a great sense of humour well evident in his after dinner talks – ' I was rushing home from a conference in Dublin one time,' he recalled, 'and Amiens Street station was packed – not a seat anywhere on the Belfast train.'

'Looking about the crowded platform I spotted a porter looking rather complacent.'

'My good man,' says I, 'I can't find a seat anywhere.'

' 'Fraid we're full for Belfast, sir.'

'Surely there's something…? I continue, before a brainwave strikes me and opening my wallet I take out a crisp £5 note and place in in his breast pocket with a friendly pat.'

'Ah!' says the porter – 'Follow me!'

'As we push through the milling crowds he turns and says, "Develop a limp"'

'What on earth I think but obey all the same.'

'But then he rebukes me saying – "You'll have to do better than that."'.'

'So there I go all but genuflecting along the platform and looking ridiculous carrying my overnight bag and briefcase as he parts the crowds for me.'

'Eventually we get to the carriage behind the engine and stuck on the door is a white paper with a red cross and the words *Medical only.*'

"Home and dry now, sir. In you go – and a pleasant journey," beams the porter.

'I step in and am shocked to find my colleagues from the conference. Like me all had developed a limp!'

A Magnificent Man *Without* His Flying Machine

Derry's Joe Cordner was one of the leading aviators in Ireland in the early days of flight. In those times pilots constructed their machines as well as flying them and as one might guess there were quite a few hair-raising episodes. Joe's first flight at Lisfannon beach around the end of the first decade of the 1900s ended with his plane crashing but gradually he got things together and local folk could see him regularly in the air around 1912. He used a field at Campsie and it is here that disaster almost struck in a sensational way. One day as he primed the propeller to start the engine he got his son to hold the machine on a rope until he could climb aboard. However, the plane revved up with such force that the lad could not hold it and off it went on its own with father and son giving chase. Early planes were so light that it was little time before lift-off and luckily only the presence of a tree stopped it from soaring skywards – the machine falling to the ground in a tangled heap..

History was to repeat itself in Nebraska decades later when a Piper aircraft took off while a mechanic was working at it. He turned to fetch something when the engine revved to speed, raced down the runway and took off on its own reaching 200 ft. before crashing into a cornfield.

Joe Cordner, the Derry Aviator died in 1963 at the age of 88 years.

Excerpts from My Diary

AUGUST 7 1958
ON TOP OF SACRE COEUR – AND A FRIGHT!

Paris – left school – freedom! Here for a week – the smell of a different world – excitement, everything new!

Today I climbed the Sacre Coeur the famous white church with the odd egg-shaped domes. on top of the hill of Montmartre

Such a shock was waiting for me – like the Psalm – 'You know my folly, oh my God!'

To get there I walked all the way through crowds of people in Montmatre – everywhere artists painting – hundreds of steps up to the church. I had heard about the magnificent mosaic of Our Lord inside the basilica so I latched onto a guide taking folk round – 'It had the biggest bell in France,' said he, 'a unique organ and over a dozen chapels, and on we trooped...

Then, as I looked around, to my left I saw a small door in the wall. Curiosity beckoned and I slipped away to find a set of narrow stone steps spiralling ever upwards. Up, up, I went until at the top I found a small hatch through which I crawled, and suddenly – can it be believed, I found myself out on the roof of Sacre Coeur – all of Paris stretched before me – Eiffel Tower in the distance and the great white dome curving skywards above me – there were two medium sized domes and two other smaller ones.

I felt that excitement and apprenshion one gets when you know you shouldn't be there. I walked about exploring the jungle of pillars and carved outcrops feeling somewhat strange. Then suddenly as I rounded a little dome there was nothing – I was on the very edge, a sheer drop – hundreds of feet below were the milling crowds. One more step and I was over – my head swam, giddiness, shock and fear possessing me on that precipitous edge. Somehow I threw myself backwards and picking myself up dashed for the hatch, descending the stone stairs two at a time until I reached the ground breathless – that was how close I was to not being.

My Guardian Angel had worked overtime!

Note: Since those far-off days visitors can now reach a viewing gallery approached on the outside of Sacre Coeur.

MAY 1960 – RATHLIN ISLAND
'SURE THE YOUNG FELLA 'ILL HAVE A DROP TOO.'

Night time in a little cottage on Rathlin Island and I scribble this before I fall over asleep, my head reeling from drinking whiskey, which I don't even like. I've only ever heard of Rathlin before today. Now at the age of 22 as engineering technician I've been posted here to maintain the new VHF radio link that enables calls to and from the island automatically. I crossed over earlier on an open motor boat with the man I'm replacing, 65 year-old Scotsman Andy Cobham. And Scotland looked so close as we sailed up past Fairhead and came down to Rathlin on the tide.

We had tea at the Post Office where all the equipment is located and met the McCurdy sisters and Joe. Naturally, it was all tears with Andy's last visit before he said to me, 'We'll go now and visit McCuaig's Pub – it's only a wee walk along the East shore.'

It was coming on to dark when we got there and all eyes fell on us as we entered – all chatter stopped. It was a dark big room with masts and ships' figureheads. The only light was a tilley lamp sitting on the bar counter so there were shadows leaping up and down everywhere. Four really big men in sou'westers were standing at the bar and looked us up and down as if we'd just come in from Mars.

'Here's hoping you've a good retirement Mr. Cobham,' said Tony McCuaig from behind the counter. 'You'll have a wee dram. Ye served us well!'

Then looking me in the eye, says he, 'Sure the young fella 'ill have a drop too.'

At this he placed a tumbler on the counter and to my dismay half-filled it with whiskey. All eyes were on me. It was like a coming of age – would Rathlin perish if I didn't drink? So I closed my eyes and downed it like a glass of water. It seemed to get the bar's approval for suddenly it was all babble and back-slapping. However, all of a sudden it was as if I were out on the sea again, the room spinning, and tossing up and down.

How I got outside I do not know. We'd reached the entry to the Post Office when Andy came up with another shock – ' I forgot to tell you

I'm stopping in the Post Office but you're up there.'

Up there was a twinkling light in a little cottage high up on the hill side that took me nearly half an hour to reach – taking both sides of the road with me as I went. The only compensation was the niceness of the cottage folk who served me hot tea and griddle cakes understanding that Rathlin's New Man was young and had still a lot to learn. So eyes heavy I make to sleep.

BOXING DAY 1962 – RATHLIN HAZARDOUS JOURNEY

Weather very cold and forecast bad – high winds. Called out to Rathlin, radio breakdown this morning and after a hazardous crossing am tucked up in a warm bed in the Post Office. They say it will rise to hurricane force and we had a touch of it on the way over – fierce. We're 100 yards from the shore here and seaweed is blowing past my window.

Actually, nearly didn't get here for when I arrived at Ballycastle 20ft. waves were breaking over the harbour wall – storm getting worse. Jack Coyle the boatman says there's no chance of crossing – it won't settle for days. As we're chatting suddenly out of the raging seas appears the Rathlin boat that comes in on a wave with the boatman shouting – 'Man ill – doctor – urgent!' With that the boat goes out on the same wave and hangs off the harbour. Within minutes a doctor is beside me with his bag – I with my radio gear. Once again the boat comes in this time against the pier wall and without considering the risk both the doctor and I jump down into it. We gather ourselves with the boat pitching – there are four crew – at the tiller the great Jimmy McCurdy tall and commanding in his sou'wester – I think folk believe he can master any conditions.

'Get under the tarpaulin!' Jimmy roars as we head into the thick of it. It was a hazardous crossing as we're thrown this way and that not knowing what's happening – but then after nearly an hour suddenly calm and peeping out miraculously we're entering Rathlin harbour.

Immediately, I dash to the radio station at the Post Office and in little time I've repaired the fault – one of the first calls out is the doctor

requesting urgent assistance. Twenty minutes later a helicopter sweeps in and lifts he ill man and the doctor – but not me!
   I'm storm bound on Rathlin!
Note: It was over a week before I got off the island. The incident made the newspapers.

SEPTEMBER 1964
MY BOOKS ARE IN THE RIVER, SIR!
My second day in teaching and a long way to finding my feet. Yesterday was straightforward – making a register, distributing brand new text books and chit chat – the boys 30 of them all just 16 years old. Hardened colleagues have no end of advice – don't turn your back at the blackboard; don't be soft on them or they'll eat you alive and don't let them know your favourite soccer team. I should be all right I tell myself – after all I've worked in industry; I've coached youngsters in soccer and cricket so what's there to fear?

   'Open your English books at Chapter 3 – it's about the story of Treasure Island,' I instruct.

   There's a rustle of pages turning – I survey the scene and am ready to start when I see a boy halfway down the class with his desk top completely empty.

   'Where are your books, young man?' I ask.

   'My books are in the river, sir! says he nonchalantly.

   'How do you mean – your books are in the river?'

   'I was leaning over the bridge and they fell in.'

   'Calm, calm,' I tell myself, and realising all eyes are on me I continue. 'Don't you realise that's school property?'

   A boy at the front says under his breath – 'He threw them in deliberately.'

   'Steady as you go,' I tell myself the class tittering away and the indifferent boy seemingly almost proud of himself.

   If in doubt ask perpetrators to report to the office I was told and so I take the easy way out – 'After class please report your loss to the secretary,' I say. 'In the meantime share your neighbour's book.'

It was as easy as that.

Later some of the boys told me it's a stunt he tries with new teachers. He's just waiting to go into a job and about to leave school.

As one might guess he never called at the office

MONDAY 15 OCTOBER 1979
BECOMING A BROADCASTER

Today, and typical of me, I've pushed myself well beyond my comfort zone. Can it be believed that I've just presented live on air Radio Foyle's morning current affairs programme – with the station just weeks old?

It beggars belief – a few weeks back I was interviewed about my efforts to keep Derry City F. C. alive and the BBC folk setting up the new Radio Foyle said I had a good voice and would I like to try some radio work. Then, last evening (Sunday 14 October), when I'd come in to the station late to try some editing the managers appeared and asked if they could have a word with me.

'What is it?' I asked.

'Our morning presenter has had an accident and we need someone for tomorrow morning's show.'

'Yes…?'

'We think you're the man for it.'

'But I've never done anything like that in my life!' I stammered.

'We'll be with you all the way – and your voice will carry you.'

In a quandary I reported at six o'clock this morning – two live and two taped interviews – the weather and the news I was told. To be honest the minutes were running that fast to 'On Air' time I just got on with it.

Then at 7:30am seated at the presenter's desk I opened the fader that fired the programme jingle, then opened my mic – 'A very good morning, this is Radio Foyle's Breakfast Programme – I'm KenMcCormack…'

Afterwards, shaken and well stirred, with hearty congratulations I went on to my work as a lecturer.

Note: I've kept up radio work for years, interviewing the great and the good, and am still at it!

DECEMBER 1979
DR. WHO'S SCARF
EVENING NEWS RADIO FOYLE

Tom Baker, a highly popular Dr. Who, visited Derry in 1978 – part of his fame was his remarkable 18ft.-long multi-coloured scarf. Later, a version of the scarf was raffled in Derry and the winner was a young boy aged about five years or so. The producer of Radio Foyle's six o'clock news bulletin thought it would be a good idea to interview the boy unaware I think of the old adage among media folk that children can present a challenge to interviewers and, believe me, I was indeed about to be challenged.

As I looked up from opening my 'mic' there sitting before me was a delightful young lad sitting on his father's knee. Dr. Who's scarf was wrapped round him and wriggled its way out of the studio disappearing somewhere off down the corridor.

'Well now, my boy, what do you think of your famous new scarf?' I asked.

There was no reply. The poor boy was absolutely overcome with his unexpected surroundings.

'Do you watch Dr. Who on the television?'

A nod of the head but no answer. On it went my pulse rising and still no response to my questions. This is how the unexpected can descend on one in radio – but then the producer attempts to come to the rescue saying in my headphones.

'Put your questions to his father.'

'So you must be delighted,' I continue, addressing the father.

The response is a smile and a nod and nothing more the poor man overwhelmed by the whole occasion.

So it goes on the atmosphere unreal until in the remaining few minutes I put the questions and answer them myself.

It didn't take away from the boy winning the Dr. Who scarf... but talking of scarves it left me feeling very hot under the collar!

SPRING 1980
A NICE LITTLE EARNER...!

Shortly after Radio Foyle moved to temporary premises in Rock Road at the start of 1980 manager Ian Kennedy meets me on the steps one evening when I called to see what possibilities there are for the 7:00 – 9:00 am programme, which I'm presenting. Ian had that look of – 'Do you want the 'big' news...or the really 'big' news?'

'Go ahead,' says I prepared for anything – the Troubles are raging.

'George Howard, Chairman of the BBC Board of Governors, is calling on us first thing tomorrow morning.'

'What!' I gasp, recalling that the highly experienced Howard – he's been eight years a governor of the BBC and owner of the fabulous Howard Castle – is not short of speaking his mind about all things BBC.

Ian continues – 'And ...he wants to be interviewed at the top of the programme.'

I gasp again for I'm still finding my feet in radio – ' He won't take any prisoners!'

Right on 7:00 am George Howard is sitting opposite me in the studio distinguished and immaculate looking. Yet he is chatty and indeed most mannerly and the interview goes off exceedingly well. Afterwards Ian collars me, 'Fine,' he chirps. 'We're having breakfast on the premises and he wants to have a chat with you.'

It was hardly going to be an invite to visit his castle but anyway it was really all small talk until he said to me 'You know Ken when I'm shaving and looking into my mirror at first light I say to myself why can't all of them *be up at this time!'*

In full flight he continues, 'I suppose you've heard ITV are filming Brideshead Revisited at my place – the castle – lights, cameras, acting folk everywhere.'

Then leaning over he whispers the amount he's getting each day for the use of the castle.

'Heavens!' I gasp once more.

'On yes! says he with a great laugh. 'Nice little earner...!'

Note: Sometime later I realised I had missed a trick. George Howard became Lord Howard in 1983 the year he retired from the BBC on grounds of ill health. What I discovered was that he was the grandson of the 9Th Earl of Carlisle. It would have been nice to tell him that his ancestor had been in Derry before him – also called George Howard, 7th Earl of Carlisle and Lord Lieutenant of Ireland who came to Derry to open Carlisle Bridge in 1863 – the bridge was named after him as was Derry's Carlisle Road.

The ITV series of *Brideshead Revisited* was first screened in1981.

22 FEBRUARY 1981
THE MAN WHO SLEPT WITH A QUEEN
On Radio Foyle evening news duty I read that an expert bee keeper is giving a talk at the White Horse Inn, A nice little piece for the morning programme I think and off I go to interview the speaker. The get-together is well attended and I draw Tom, the speaker, to the side – he had a fascinating country accent and witty with it too, Just before we finish he leans over and says with a grin – 'I slept with a queen, you know.'

"You slept with a queen!' I gasp amazed.

'I surely did – a queen bee of course.'

'Ah! And how did you manage that?'

'I put her in this wee cage and slip her into my pyjama pocket – for warmth.'

The cage was about the size of a walnut and had little slits.

'You don't!' says I. 'What does your wife say when she finds you're sleeping with a queen?'

'Not a thing, She just turns over and goes to sleep! The bee's happy and so am I.'

SUMMER 1982 – LISFANNON
ON THE BEACH WITH JOSEF LOCKE
Idling on the beach, just past Fahan, County Donegal, this afternoon, who should pull up beside me but Josef Locke who is now living at

nearby Burnfoot. We sit and chat while his wife Carmel takes the dog for a walk – a recent performance of his in Derry's Guildhall gets an airing – he wasn't too happy about the outcome. This was now a more subdued 'Jo' – no surprise after the life of stardom that was his for decades. When one thinks of it he was unmatched – Blackpool seasons, radio, television, films and musicals. He'd done the London Palladium, Royal Variety Performances – even sang for Princess Diana and I suppose, one must add, led a colourful life as well. Yet one thing I like about 'Jo' apart from his magnificent voice is his 'presence'. Audiences loved him and part of his giant personality is the twinkle in his eye.

However, on this day looking at the beauty of Inch Island and Lough Swilly as we reflect on the ways of the world all the adulation, all the applause, all his famous friends in show business, all that is behind him.

One of the things I've learned in top performers I've had the privilege to know is that 'off stage' so to speak they keep their brilliance to themselves – their stardom waits until they go before the 'lights'.

'The wonderful Donegal scenery has put him at ease,' I thought.

Nonetheless what a thrill to be in his company on this summer afternoon beside the magical Lake of Shadows.

Note: Josef Locke – Joseph Mc Laughlin, of Derry, died in October 1999 aged 82.

AUGUST 1985
SEVENTH SON OF A SEVENTH SON

'…and would you believe, sir, the crutches went leapin' after her…!'

Today I've been in the heart of County Antrim interviewing a seventh son of a seventh son for my series of programmes on Healers for Radio Ulster. I found myself on a long road with a sprinkling of government cottages and had no trouble finding him.

'Come in and welcome,' says he.

Daniel was a remarkable man – small, sharply featured and most certainly sharp-eyed. He was wearing a flat cap and had a dark suit and collar and tie. Straightaway I could tell he was a solid and genuine human being.

He led me into a sparsely furnished parlour in the front of the cottage – a table against the wall had a chair at each side and two large books that I could see were bibles. On the wall there was a religious picture with a biblical quotation and the floor was covered in linoleum.

'Before we start', adds he, with a glint in his eye, 'I'm the seventh son of a seventh son man and boy.'

Then to the bibles on the table.

'You see the two bibles on this table – one's for Catholics and t'other's for Protestants. The Good Lord welcomes all.'

I found him lively and chatty as he went over all his times with folk coming for 'healing'.

And he had a great turn of wit, which was at its best as we parted – 'I was at the door one day,sir, when I saw this woman draggin' herself up that road on two crutches – would've taken tears from a stone. Says I, sit down there daughter we'll put an end to this. We'll I laid on hands – an' I'll tell you this – the woman went dancing down that road – and would you believe, sir, the crutches went leapin' after her...!'

Note: As part of the series I was delighted to interview the famous healer Finbar Nolan. He came across as polite, gentle and genuine. Finbarr (now deceased) had achieved celebrity status internationally – even medical folk took an interest in his healing, which in Ireland is often referred to as the '*Cure*'. It is no exaggeration to say that in his day he was a sensation.

'Can't explain it,' he said to me modestly, 'I don't even know at the time. I'm just blessed with a wonderful gift.'

SUMMER 2005 – PARIS
THE REMARKABLE CECILY MACKWORTH

What an enjoyable afternoon we've had today in the company of Cecily Mackworth journalist and novelist. Cecily was the sister of the tragic Helen Mackworth who died in the Carrigans shootings on 26 September 1938. While researching the affair we'd discovered Cecily was still alive and living in a pied-à-terre in a small courtyard off Rue de Rivoli in Paris – she was a hale and hearty 94 year-old. Our mission was to see if she had any recollections of the tragedy – so writing colleague Frank McGurk and I and his wife Audrey were all ears.

Firstly, this is a truly extraordinary woman. Cecily came from a well-off Welch family and after study took up writing and journalism. She travelled widely in Europe, Palestine and Algeria and for a time settled in France mixing with the famous writers of the day in cafes such as Le Procope and Les Deux Magots where she got to know the author Henry Miller (Tropic of Cancer) and wrote several books on French poets. Cecily witnessed the Germans marching into Paris on June 14, 1940 and fled to London to work with General de Gaul and the Free French. After World War II she travelled to Palestine and witnessed the birth of the state of Israel. Finally she married a French marquis and, though she didn't boast about it, was then a marchioness.

Petite and full of life it was a joy to chat with her – such experience, such modesty and charm of personality. She had not been in touch with her sister Helen for a while and only found out about the shocking shooting tragedy when reading news headlines at a newspaper kiosk in Switzerland. Nonetheless, being with her added to our research and after a few hours we parted from her with great sadness. I thoroughly enjoyed her delightful orange wine and was thrilled when she signed one of her books for me.

Note: Cecily died a year later in 2006

MAY 19 2016 – CHINA
THE GOLDEN BUDDHA AND ME
I've already been to Beijing and Shanghai and have come to Hangzhou with hope that I might get access to Hangzhou's most famous Buddhist shrine, the Lingyin Temple. Originally built in AD 326, it has been rebuilt no fewer than 16 times. The Great Hall contains a magnificent 20m-high statue sculpted from 24 blocks of camphor wood but the Golden Buddha statue in the courtyard – yes, it is gold and at over

30ft. in height simply takes the breath away. Incidentally, Marco Polo described Hangzhou with its pagodas and scenes straight out of the Willow Pattern as the finest and most splendid city in the world.

The temple and its monastery are regarded as among the greatest in China.

It's not everyone who gets access to Lingyin temple and its inner workings – but I did. It came about thanks to the father of a student that I'd helped get into university. When he heard I was in China he sent word he'd like to meet me in Hangzhou. Off we went in his posh car and at all the security checks on the way we were waved straight through – something I didn't fail to notice.

Standing and looking up at the Golden Buddha gives such an awesome feeling – there were one or two worshippers about – some lighting tapers, others prostrating themselves, The whole scene was extraordinary to say the least. Yet it wasn't over for me. My host whispered that the abbot had agreed to meet me. Off we were led down endless corridors in the ancient monastery until we got to a room with a very large wooden Buddha. The abbot, a youngish looking man in a light brown robe appeared and bade us be seated for there were a number of people in the room. I sat on one side of the Buddha and he on the other. He had travelled and could speak good English and so I learned all about the monastery – its history and rich cultural legacy and who better than he to explain what Buddhism was all about. Then he invited me to lunch in the monks refectory after which we toured around all the ancient shrines. I was absolutely astonished to see the hall of the Four Heavenly Kings and stunned with the Hall of the Five Hundred Arhats – rows of life-sized statues of revered holy men who'd worshipped here during the centuries of its existence.

Lingyin has that special presence one gets in places of selfless worship – like great shrines such as Lourdes and Fatima – unforgettable.

Acknowledgements

With this being the final volume in the Derry series I want to thank all those who have helped me with the tales over the years. Firstly, my parents Phyllis and John, and brothers Bernard and John – all of them storytellers and on the mark with folk tales near and far and I'm proud to be part of what they were about. To the late Sean McMahon, whom I considered a great friend and mentor and who really was the inspiration for the series of Derry tales, I trust the three volumes will contribute to fond memories of him. A special word also to Pauline Ross for her encouragement and many wonderful hours doing drama at the Playhouse. Also to Joe Mahon, Westway Films, and Caitríona McLaughlin, Artistic Director, Abbey Theatre, Dublin.

Ian Kennedy and Kieran Gill both excellent men of Radio Foyle offered wonderful support as did the various editors of the Derry Journal and Belfast Telegraph. Libraries are essential and here I want to acknowledge the assistance from Central Library Foyle Street, the Waterside Library and Linenhall Library Belfast. To all broadcasting colleagues at BBC Radio Foyle and BBC Northern Ireland who I have worked with for decades and who have helped get the stories 'on air' my thanks. My appreciation to Gerald Harvey of the Foyle Family History Society who offered me such great support in so many ways and to David Jenkins who combed many a newspaper archive for me. Time and time again Pearse Henderson of Eglinton produced marvellous historical gems for me and to the many others who brought me stories goes my grateful thanks. My old friend Richie Kelly and I travelled the highways and byways together and shared great stories on the way – much appreciated.

To my great friend Frank McGurk, a fine talent, my thanks for the countless hours of enjoyment we spent on the 'Dunmore' tale. Nor can I forget the endless roads that my broadcasting colleagues Colum Arbuckle, Deidre Donnelly, Mark Patterson and I spent in search of unearthing local tales – likewise Stanley Page who has a feel for unique yarns. I must not forget to mention the enthusiasm and support of the members of the many committees I have served on especially – Friends of Prehen, the Hervey Heritage Society and the St. Columb's Park History Group. To Sean McAnnaney, Joey Zhou and Frank Harkin who frequently helped me goes my thanks; also, a special appreciation to Jim Hunter, Loretto Blackwood and Jerry Sayers as we pursued the Earl Bishop and not forgetting Frank Carey, the late Annesley Malley and the late Roy Hamilton, Peter Hamilton, Stephen Doherty, Ian Bartlett, and Ivor Doherty of the Derry Tower Group.

Last is not least great – thanks to Diana Kilpatrick who beavered away at editing volume III for me – most appreciated. Also, to Mark McConnellogue who helped put the manuscript together for me.

Finally, it has been a privilege to work with Ken Thatcher, *Foyle Books* and Garbhán Downey the publisher of *Colmcille Press*. They've helped so much to make the Derry books possible and I'm most grateful.

Gallery

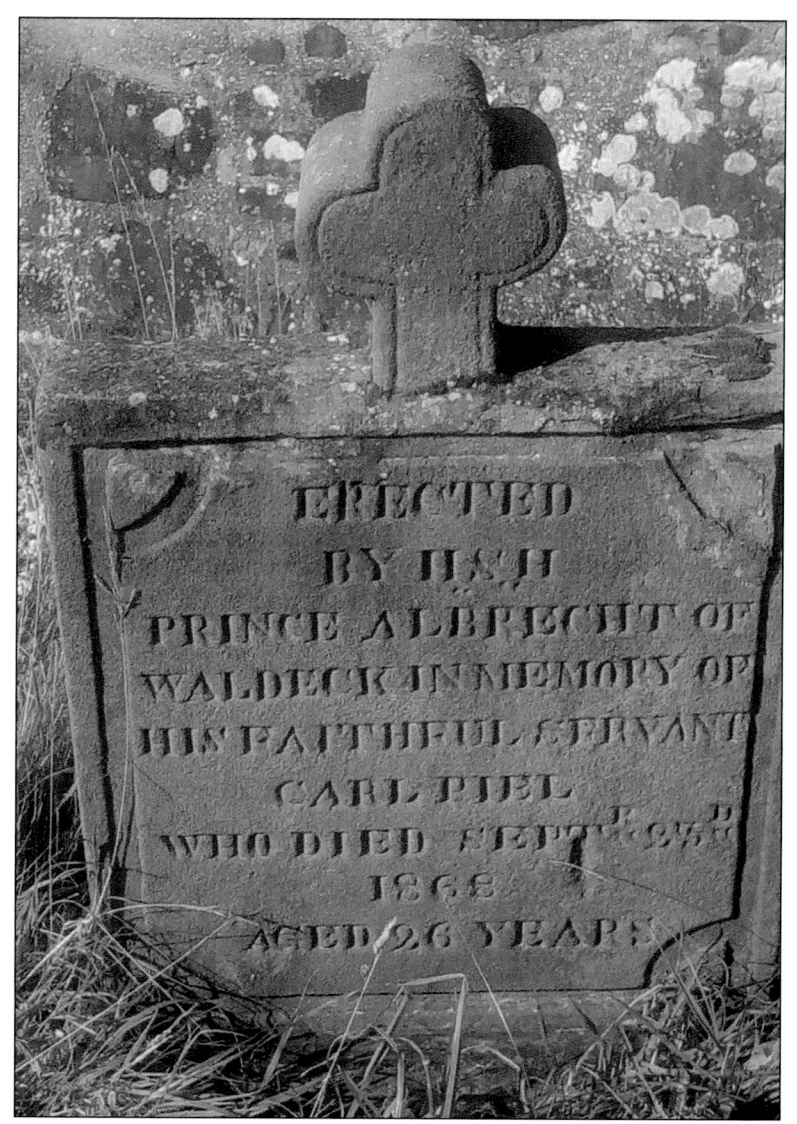

Carl Piel's Grave on Rathlin Island

Geoffrey Hill, the Enagh Aviator

Captain Erik Kokeritz and his ship SS Rochester

BBC Headlines in Psychic News

Madame Beck and Husband Ernst

The *Lyster Jackson* – Lyster Jackson Homemade Car

Aeneas Coffey –
The Whiskey Man

Lord Leitrim – Third Earl

Manor Vaughan House

The Honourable
H.V. Strutt

St. Columb's Park House

Carlisle Bridge. Opened By the Seventh Earl of Carlisle (1863)

Above: Old Glendermott Graveyard – Site of the Ivy Church

Left: The Cricketer's Grave (Samuel Donnell)

Ballerina Ailne Philips (Left) with Dame
Ninette de Valois (centre) and Friend

MISS AILNE PHILLIPS.

Owencarrow Viaduct Disaster (30th January 1925)

Tom Baker
(Doctor Who and
the Famous Scarf)

Sir Ian Fraser, Surgeon – Develop a Limp!